Time Is of the Essence

Time Is of the Essence

How to Create More Time in a Stress-Filled World

Edith del Mar Behr MD

iUniverse LLC
Bloomington

TIME IS OF THE ESSENCE
How to Create More Time in a Stress-Filled World

iUniverse books may be ordered through booksellers or by contacting:

iUniverse LLC
1663 Liberty Drive
Bloomington, IN 47403
www.iuniverse.com
1-800-Authors (1-800-288-4677)

ISBN: 978-1-4759-9466-7 (sc)
ISBN: 978-1-4759-9468-1 (hc)
ISBN: 978-1-4759-9467-4 (e)

Library of Congress Control Number: 2013910825

Printed in the United States of America.

iUniverse rev. date: 02/19/2014

Contents

This book is dedicated to my sister, Maria, who is now
in spirit supporting me and encouraging me in all my
passionate endeavors through my connection with The Divine

Introduction

There is a way to enter a new relationship with time and make it work for you. There is a way that you can walk through life, never feeling rushed for time. There is a way to feel as if you have more than enough time for family, work, and play. There is a way to have unlimited time for passionate endeavors. There is a way for you to find time expanding to accommodate your life. There is a way to feel as if you are on vacation every day, with unlimited time for relaxation and fun activities—and the knowledge that you are so deserving of this.

The fact that you are reading this tells me that you have bought into the illusion that time is real and that you don't have enough of it. In fact, time is a product of your mind and perception, and you have as much time as you want. You control or can control your mind, how you perceive time, and how you "spend" your time. Learning how to do this is easy and can be done in a variety of ways, all of which are addressed in this writing. It does not matter how or where you want to start.

As a surgeon in private practice, I once felt that there wasn't enough time in the day to get it all done—let alone enjoy my family and passions. It finally hit me that I had arrived at a place where the next break in the action would be retirement, which meant twenty to thirty more years of what I was living. In addition, by the time I retired, I might not have been able to enjoy my passions and certainly would have missed many family moments. Would my parents be alive by then? Would my children live near me? Would I be healthy enough to dance the way I love to dance?

The thought of living even twenty years feeling that I was in a race and not seeing any finish line was not acceptable. Unfinished business, deadlines, chart work, obligations with family and work, neglected personal desires—these all seemed to be constant threads in the back of my mind. There were enjoyable moments sprinkled here and there, but for some reason, I believed that was how life was supposed to be. Struggle and work with an occasional pleasurable reward was the model that seemed to prevail in the world I lived in.

I could go on about how it used to be, but I want to get to how it *can* be. In a few short months after making the decision that living my life like most of us live our lives was not acceptable, I found a way to live the dream.

I read every self-help book I could get my hands on. I listened to audio programs. I went to conferences about self-improvement. I found amazing concepts hidden within all of it that changed my life in a miraculous way. I also found that I had to be vigilant about self-help, because each and every one of us has our own path. Luckily, I had reached my saturation point for other people telling me how it should be.

The key to my success in this endeavor is that I read and listened to all viewpoints—but I only accepted what felt good to me. No one, including me, is the expert on *your* life and path. When someone said I must journal and I wasn't inspired to journal, I didn't. In fact, the last thing I was looking for was another task to add to my daily list. In the end, just by changing my thoughts, I changed my life—without effort. I found that time expanded not because I was trying to expand it, but rather it simply expanded when I relaxed and lived the moment I was in.

I started getting more done in a day—with less effort. My office ran on time; how often do you find that in a busy doctor's practice? I was able to "play mom" while having a career—without difficulty. People showed up in my life who enjoyed doing what I didn't want to do, and they did it better than I would have done it. I found that every day felt like a vacation. No work or effort was involved.

The other great thing about the methods that I will reveal to you is that, as you begin to take control of your time, you begin to get positive reinforcement from the universe in the form of miraculous time gifts. There is no adjustment period, no time when you have to endure exercises and discomfort to get to the prize. There is no hard work, journaling, or diet you must follow. You can't do it wrong unless you *want* to do it wrong; even then, you must try very hard to accomplish this.

So, as you go through all of the components of my methods, realize that there is no order of importance. All of the necessary concepts and abilities build upon each other. They are so interrelated that, even if you leave something out, that component will find a way to associate with one of the other components. In other words, the intention to make time work for you will make it happen. You cannot fail at this unless you choose to fail—and you will also learn how *not* to choose failure.

Chapter One

Entertain the Possibility

For starters, open yourself to the possibility that you have as much time as you need; in fact, you have as much time as you want for everything you want to do. Entertain the idea that every thought you have is creating the reality you experience. You don't have to believe this at the moment, but try living as if you do, and the proof will be in what you experience.

What do I mean by living as if you believe your every thought creates your reality? Well, to understand this concept, you have to become *aware*. Become aware of what you are saying to yourself and the world in every moment. Can you remember what you were thinking before you began to read this? Can you remember what you were thinking about yourself when you looked in the mirror this morning while you brushed your teeth? What did you think about sitting behind the car in front of you at the red light? What did you say to yourself (or think) about your spouse, your children, a friend, a coworker, a woman walking down the street with very tight pants, your boss, etc.? Of course, if the woman in tight pants is your boss, that is for another book . . . he he.

Seriously, though, if your thoughts tend toward being critical of yourself and others, you are setting yourself up to find more work. You have sentenced yourself to spend each moment in a less-than-relaxed and appreciative state, but a relaxed and appreciative state is where time expands. In addition, on a more practical level, if you are overcritical, you won't find anyone in your life who can do the jobs you don't want to do well enough. You also won't find time to enjoy yourself, because you have a list of corrections to make before you can love yourself.

Imagine if every thought instantly manifested in reality and you were thinking about how your computer could get a virus, how signs of old age are starting to appear on your face, how the guy in front of you is driving like a jerk and it would serve him right if he got into an accident. Imagine if all that came true, instantly, right before your eyes. I think we would all be more careful about what we were thinking if we saw right before our eyes the computer freeze up, more wrinkles and gray hair appear, and the guy in front of us get into an accident, resulting in our spending a few hours stopped in traffic.

It just so happens that this *is* how it works. It may not seem so sudden, but given the fact that you think between sixty thousand and eighty thousand thoughts a day, consciously, and that you are subconsciously feeding yourself an even greater amount of data and forming alliances with all kinds of groups and people who bleed into your data banks, it seems very complex. The fact is, however, that it is very simple. All of that thought is creating your every experience. If I am wrong, so what? But if I am right—and I am—then what are you creating with your incredibly powerful mind? Wouldn't you like to harness that power?

When you think about your computer freezing up, you also have many counter-thoughts about how your computer doesn't freeze up all the time. You have many more memories of when it works fairly well; these counteract that immediate conscious thought of disaster. That is a good thing—but just imagine if you could get all your conscious and unconscious thinking to align with what you want, *and only what you want.* That is the goal; it is also how successful people in any endeavor get where they want to go. No action in the world can counteract thoughts that are out of alignment with what you want.

Once you become aware of thoughts that work against you, you have the power to change those thoughts, statements, and beliefs to what you would like to live and experience. For example, thinking or saying, "I don't have enough time" would be changed to "I have plenty of time." I know, right now you are saying, "I thought she said this would be easy." Keep reading with that in mind, and I will make it easy for you.

In reference to the time issue, instead of saying, "I don't have time to do this or that," change the internal dialogue to "I choose not to spend my time doing this or that." This puts you in a position to take control of your life—instead of letting life drag you along a path you do not want. If you want to have plenty of time for everything, you have to stop telling yourself that you don't have time for things you want.

In a bigger sense, you have to stop telling the universe that you have no time. The universe, or little people, or whatever it is that makes this a force that works as systematically as gravity, grants your every wish. There is no judgment about whether it is good for you or not, just pure response. You may not believe it but, just for now, entertain the possibility and act as if it is so. Just for now, become aware of the messages you are giving the universe, or yourself, to carry out.

First and foremost, if you continue to say out loud and to yourself that you don't have enough time, you will continue to create that truth in your world. For example, if you continue to want to exercise but do not, stop using the excuse that you don't have time, and state clearly in your mind that you are choosing not to exercise. In reality, you know that you have time, but you have made other choices, such as sleeping or cooking dinner or cleaning or watching TV or talking on the phone—none of these are invalid choices or wrong choices. Just get clear that you have *chosen* not to exercise, and stop pretending that you don't have time.

You may have an uneasy feeling about this; I have just taken away your valid excuse for not exercising, and you are so comfortable with the excuse that you don't have enough time that you are unwilling to let that excuse go easily. It seems so real when you repeat it to yourself and others daily for years; it seems that it can't be a lie—but it is. It is a lie that seems to give you some room to breathe, but in actuality, it is cutting your life force away.

I am sure that there are moments when you are doing nothing during the day—moments when you could drop down and do twenty sit-ups. You choose otherwise because you would be embarrassed to do that at work or while waiting in line at the grocery store. You may even take the elevator when you could use the stairs. I am not making a judgment or even suggesting that you take the stairs, but I am trying to make it clear that, at every moment, you are making choices. In every moment, you are creating; if you continue to use the "I don't have enough time" excuse, you will continue to create not having enough time. Of course, that excuse will then start bleeding into all parts of your life. You will find, as you probably already do, that you don't have enough time.

In addition, when you stop proclaiming to the powers that be that you don't have enough time, and you still find that you are not doing something in your life like exercising, then you can evaluate the whole idea of exercise in your life. I use exercise as an example, but feel free to substitute anything. Is exercising what you really want to do? Or is it something you think you "should" do? The word "should" in your inner thoughts is a red flag for you to really give the issue some thought and get clear about what is important and real to you.

Maybe, instead of exercise, you want to dance, do yoga, do tai chi, or garden. Maybe you have no interest in exercise. That is okay as well. It is better to start with the truth and shape it for yourself than to let a self-fulfilling prophesy take over your entire life without your conscious consent. You will find that just living life with passion increases your energy expenditure and fitness level. You may not even have to formally exercise, but, as you get joyful, there will be a spring in every step you take—that is a lot of steps. Don't let well-meaning people or society take your power. Make your own choices in all things— including whether you exercise or choose not to exercise. You do not have to justify your choices to anyone, including and especially to yourself. If you are not doing it, then it is not for you at this moment, and there is nothing wrong with that. "Exercising" is not the only way to be thin, fit, and healthy.

Internal dialogues have an incredible power, as do external dialogues. We use them as if we are children with a loaded gun, without knowledge of its power or danger. We end up shooting ourselves in the foot, or worse, and then wonder what went wrong. It is the same with the thought of not having enough time. Change your thoughts so that you put yourself in the driver's seat. Even if you don't believe that you have enough time, continue to tell yourself that you do. In every instance that you begin by thinking or telling someone that you don't have enough time, catch yourself and rephrase it. Say to yourself or others that you have enough time and you have chosen to do something else or you have chosen to do nothing. If someone asks you to do a favor or get involved in an activity, give him or her the truth—or say nothing at all. Do not say that you don't have time. You don't have to explain yourself, and most will not question you. If you are questioned and care not to go into details, the response "for personal reasons" usually works well and sometimes causes an air of mystery—and mystery is always fun.

You will learn a lot about yourself when you realize that you have been *choosing* to not have enough time all along. Usually, there is some fear behind this choice, but take heart, as you can now learn to choose differently. Begin by acknowledging that you are making a choice in every instance; if you don't like the choice, follow the gunpowder trail. You have chosen because of some misguided belief, out of guilt or fear, or you have given your power away to another person or group of people: your family, your spouse, your boss, your church, your society, or your bowling league. Sometimes it is as simple as seeing this consciously. Other times, even though you may see a fear of loss, fear of change, or fear of success as the culprit, it may seem more complicated. In actuality, it is as complicated or as uncomplicated as we want it to be. This book will give you a simple way to find the real you in all your magnificence. I am all about no pain, definite gain.

Just becoming aware, at some level, that you are the source of your experience changes your view of that experience. It becomes an adventure into your inner self, the workings of your mind, and your subconscious motivations. It becomes an exciting game that you will, sooner or later, master. The game is one you will eventually win, no matter who you are. It is simply a matter of how long you want to play by someone else's rules—or, rather, how long you want to play without knowing the rules. At some point in your existence, you will know, without a doubt, that you make up the rules for your game and then attract those who will play by your rules—or those who have the same rules.

I can't count the number of times people in my life have changed their behavior around me just because I thought differently. This means that I changed some of my beliefs as well. I personally think that having less annoying and irritating behavior around me and more cooperative, helpful, fun people is a plus. The fact that they were the same people, transformed, was the miraculous part. Very interesting, isn't it? When you change what you believe and how you think, the circumstances of your life change to mirror those beliefs and thoughts.

Most of us are playing someone else's game by his or her rules. In fact, the ones who are making the rules may have already moved on to the next plane of existence or changed the rules for themselves. They may have been people you loved or respected or considered authorities about life.

We propagate someone else's rules by adopting them as our own; those rules then take on a life of their own. The beauty is that all you need to do is recognize them for what they are, and they will no longer have power over you or your life. The easiest way to get rid of an old rule is to put a new rule or belief in its place.

The first step is to entertain the idea that you are the power behind what is going on in your life and that, up to this point, you didn't know how to harness and use that power. In opening your mind to the possibility that you could change your life for the better without effort, you will find that it will happen.

Most would have you believe that it takes action and changing your evil ways to be successful and get what you want. This is so very far from the truth. In fact, if someone tells you something that makes you feel less than spectacular, simply ignore that person. If it is me, then ignore me. There is no effort in being successful. Even though, as you lose the baggage that made you think you were less than magnificent, you may engage in activities that seem industrious, you will feel like that activity is flowing and easy. You will also feel that you have plenty of time to do whatever it is you want to do and doing what you love leads to a very successful life on all levels.

When I began this process in 1996, I used two logical assumptions to support my new thoughts. One was that if this is not true, then I am sentenced to my life as it is—and why would I want that? This made me want to accept the premise that I am the power behind my life. The other logical assumption was that the idea that our thoughts create our experience is the only explanation for the random appearance of life. This idea explains how one person can do something and get an entirely different result from another person doing the same thing. It is the only fair way the world could work in what appears to be an unfair existence.

We could get into a bunch of data and quantum physics about the whole idea, but all you have to do is entertain the possibility that it is true; apply yourself to thinking differently, and the proof will be in your experience. It is supposed to be that simple.

Chapter Two

Becoming Aware

Another component of making time work for you is becoming aware of how you spend your time. This has nothing to do with *doing* anything about it; just become conscious of why you do the things you do.

Start observing yourself, your life, who controls it, and what purpose your actions serve. Are the activities you do the activities you want to do? Are they activities that you feel you must do? Are they things you do to forget or ignore your life? Do *you* choose, or does someone else choose? During this process, you are merely observing yourself and where your time "goes." Observe how you make decisions about what you do or don't do. There are some who feel they have no decision to make, that most of their actions are chosen for them, or that they spend a lot of time putting out fires or rushing to the next activity that is, of course, a necessity.

When you are not "doing" anything, what do you feel? Do you "waste" time? Why? Do you feel guilt over wasting time? What activities or nonactivities are in your "wasting time" category, and how did you come to that decision? What are your beliefs about wasting time? Do you take time for yourself regularly, or do you do it sparingly and then feel guilty? Must you fill your every waking moment with something to do, watch, or play? Do you actually know what you want to do, what gives you joy, and what activities you are passionate about? Becoming aware of all of this does not take any time; it just requires a different thought pattern.

Instead of allowing life to go on without you, become a part of it—become aware of what makes you tick, function, go through the motions, and why. Don't be frustrated if you can't be aware all the time or if your questions to yourself have no answers. The answers and solutions will come to you when you can handle them, and we will get to that as well. Above all, have fun with it, try not to judge, and be patient with yourself. This is just a data-gathering experience. It is not meant to be a beating-up-on-yourself experience. We are all in the same boat, trying to figure out how to steer the darn thing.

Actually, life is very simple when you get rid of all of the baggage you are carrying around. If you were living heaven on earth, you wouldn't be reading this, and you would already be aware of your every desire. You would be in touch with who you are and what you want. You would be manifesting the life you want, in the company of the people you want to be with. This is what you can experience; but first, you must become aware of how you spend your time and why.

Are you following someone else's desires? Your parents' desires? Society's desires? Do you defer to other people's choices because you don't want to deal with their anger or hurt? Do you follow the crowd? Do you feel obligated to attend functions that end in the word "shower," like a bridal shower or baby shower, even though you may not know the "showeree" well? Do your children's activities seem to consume 90 percent of your time? Do you get roped into things because of guilt? Do you get roped into things in quest of an ever-changing idea of perfection? Do you think you are the only one who can do certain things correctly? Do you feel that someone else or circumstances are to blame when you are rushed beyond your comfort level? Do you get into bed at night thinking of all the things you have to do? Does it seem that, no matter what you do, you never get ahead? Do you even know what you need to "get ahead" of? Did you ever wonder if it would truly make you happy to have plenty of time to do all of the things that you think you have to do? Or have you filled your life with things you would rather not do, using the stress of your lack of time to hide the truth from yourself? Please read the last statement again if you didn't clearly understand it. Entertain the idea that you may be using your "lack of time" as an excuse in case you fall short of your expectations or as a way to hide from your true purpose.

Your true purpose is to be wildly happy and have any and all experiences you desire. You don't have to save the world or the whales—unless that makes you wildly happy and is what you desire. When you are living *this* moment with exquisite joy and love, you do more for the whole universe than if you spent five lifetimes sacrificing to help others less fortunate. Okay, maybe ten to twenty lifetimes; the math has yet to be determined.

Don't spend time evaluating or comparing your life with anyone else's life in this process; it will not help you figure out how to have more time. You can't evaluate another person's life and know whether he or she is doing it right; you can't follow someone else's example. This is what we have been doing forever, but there is a major flaw in that method—maybe two or three major flaws. One is that we are all completely unique; one person's poison is another person's gourmet meal. Second, what makes someone successful is not an outside job, so, no matter how many blind people are feeling the elephant and comparing notes, they will never define the elephant. Even if they come up with the picture of an elephant, they are not getting what makes it work. Third, we are in a world that constantly changes, so the recent past does not work in the present—no matter how much we think we want it to. In other words, stick to yourself and what makes you sing, tick, cringe, cry, laugh. You are unique. There is nothing you can see from the outside of someone else, as in what the person is doing, that can help you, and you can't get inside anyone else's head.

What does this have to do with becoming aware of what makes you tick?

I asked myself that same question. We are all very attached to what our parents think or some modification of it, what the society we live in thinks, the opinions of the groups we belong to, and our friends' and relatives' ideas of what is right. As a result, we give our power away, both consciously and unconsciously. In reality, we needed our parents when we were infants, and we've allowed that dependence to continue, unchallenged. This dependence is no longer necessary. None of these groups can take anything away from you unless you give it to them. That is the reality, and to the degree that you see that clearly in your mind and heart, that is the degree of freedom you will have. If you have not had an aha moment or epiphany, don't worry—it is coming soon.

You will find that, when you stop needing someone else's approval, someone will approve of you. It may even be the person who was disapproving of you. You know that you still need approval when a person close to you disapproves of you. That is how it works. If someone is giving you a hard time and disapproval, look within. There will be a tiny part of you that is screaming, "I don't think I am worthy!" or "I feel this might be wrong!" You worry that, if someone disapproves of you, you will feel less worthy. When you finally get to the place where you don't care what others think, then no one will question you.

When I was a resident, I got pregnant and had a beautiful baby boy. Now, a resident works a hundred or more hours a week, being on call. My mom stayed home and was a firm supporter of breast-feeding. In my mind, my son had to be breast-fed for me to feel okay with being a working mom. There was absolutely *no doubt* in my mind that this was right. Many women residents might complain about the men being unsupportive, but I found that every man, woman, and administrator bent over backward for me to be able to breast-feed my son while I worked that many hours. When you have no doubt that you are doing the right thing, no one gets in your way. If someone is getting in your way, then look inside, and you will see your own doubts attracting the circumstance.

Become aware of why you do what you do and to whom you have given your amazing power. Own your ability to create your own reality, and use the mirror of life to direct you to the places where you have been leaking power. When you take your power back, you will find that there is always plenty of time for everything.

Chapter Three

Imagine, Imagine, Imagine

Now that you are becoming aware of who you are and what "makes" you do the things you do, use that new awareness: take those moments when you are delayed or waiting, and use them to imagine something beautiful and pleasant. When you are waiting in line, stuck in traffic, picking up a child from an activity, attending a boring meeting, watching a commercial on TV, or delayed in any way, use that gift to imagine what you would like to be doing. Imagine something real—or something gloriously fantastic. Start developing a story that makes you feel great when you think about it, and think about that, instead of thinking about things that make you feel not so great or downright anxious, angry, or sad. Just that small amount of pleasurable daydreaming will change life for you, if you get into the habit of doing it. You will feel so good doing it that the habit will become its own reward.

If you are blessed to know what you would love to do "if you had the time," begin imagining those activities in your life. Imagine how it would feel to do them. Imagine ways you could do them—and what you would have to do to start. For example, if you love to dance, imagine taking a dance class or joining a dancing group. Then imagine you are a famous dancer who makes more money than you know what to do with! If you would love to have your own business, imagine the business; imagine what proportions this business would take if you had no limitations. If you want to be a retired, wealthy philanthropist, then imagine sitting on the beach outside your beautiful beach house, writing a check to some worthy cause as you sip your margarita.

Imagine what you think is possible; then imagine the impossible, and try to imagine the feeling you would have doing it, being it, and living it. Remember, I can't tell you what makes you feel good, what is better than sex when you think about it—only you can. Start playing with some ideas in your head. The only criteria are that imagining it should feel great and you should be in it—not watching yourself in it like a movie. If you are imagining your dream and feeling less than great, you need to get in touch with what you truly want, or make your daydream less detailed. If you find yourself getting distracted from your imagined idea of your life, try to make it shorter. It only needs to be seventeen seconds or more, and you can rerun it over and over again.

Imagination, associated with emotion and feelings, is a key to making things happen in your life. Use your imagination to pretend that you are already living the life of your dreams. Become only as detailed in your imaginings as you can feel good about. The key is in feeling good while imagining. If you want to have your own business, think about your daily existence: Will you have someone else do your shopping? Will you have a cleaning lady? Will you wear certain clothes? Children are very adept at this sort of imagination from an early age because it is a natural and important process. It is a shame that most of us have to relearn the art by the time we are adults and that we have all failed to see how important and pleasurable it is. In fact, pleasure is something we have come to believe we must earn and wait for—a misbelief that is so very far from the truth.

Pretend that you are living your dream life, and make as much of it reality as you can allow yourself to. For example, you may be able to dress the part. Would you feel more beautiful or special? How would you feel going into the mall? Have fun with this incredible game called life. Pretend that you are driving the car of your dreams. Assume that people are excited to see you walk into their establishment. Walk as if every person of the opposite gender is turning around to get a look at you (unless you are gay, of course; modify as appropriate).

It is vitally important to develop your own dramas. Someone may want to be a leading scientist or be considered incredibly intelligent. Someone else may want to be very wealthy or to cure the world of hunger. The point is to imagine and cultivate the feelings associated with the ideas you imagine. Have fun, which is also another point—or perhaps the actual point. When you are enjoying the moment, time expands.

Most important, identify what concerns and fears are associated with the activity or life you desire. This matters because, believe it or not, these are the real reasons that you don't "have time" to do those activities, to live that life. What concerns have you created to stop you from getting to where you want to go? You heard me correctly—it is your own walls, fears, and insecurities that are keeping you from what you want and nothing else. Your fears are what keep you from having plenty of time.

We fill our lives with mundane and unnecessary activities or we "waste" time doing nothing, as if an outside force immobilizes us. Why? Because deep down, we fear doing what we love or don't think we deserve to do it. It seems much "safer" to do what has been done before and follow what everyone else seems to be doing. It seems ironic to take comfort in doing things the way they have been done before when all through our existence, things keep changing. That is the only constant that exists in our physical world—change.

We spend all our energy trying to swim up the river where we came from, when it is inevitably going to take us downstream. Instead, we can turn around and guide ourselves down the river branch we want to travel. We will use less energy, have much more time, and get to places we are not only interested in seeing along the way but wanted to go in the first place. Not only that, but we will be turned in the direction to actually see them instead of arriving backward in the effort to avoid what we want. Seems silly to avoid what we actually want, doesn't it? Subconsciously and consciously, though, we are all doing just that, out of a misguided conviction that if it feels good, it must be wrong, bad, or fattening. That belief creates that reality.

Living the rest of your life the way everyone else has is not safe at all. In fact, if you are anywhere near clear-sighted, you will see that the world is changing, has always been changing, and the way things have been done in the past is at best outdated and in truth dangerous to your health and spirit. Life must be invented uniquely in each person's mind. That is why I am asking you to imagine how you want your life to be. When you engage in that activity instead of allowing your fears to be the dominant thoughts, then time expands, and you rendezvous with the people and events that make your dreams a reality. What is the point in having all the time in the world if you can't use the time to do what you want?

Chapter Four

Following the Selfish Road

Developing the ability to imagine our dream life brings you to the next step, which is to give yourself permission to do that which you love. You do not have to earn the right. Contrary to the collective belief that life is supposed to be a struggle, you were put here on the earth to do what you love. That's why you love it. Again, this doesn't take any time; it simply requires a change in the way you think.

It is not only your *right* to do what you love but your *mission*. Doing what you love is not only the best and healthiest thing you can do for yourself, it is also the best and healthiest thing you could do for all of humanity. The ironic thing about doing what you love is that it will give you more time in your life. Oh, and by the way, doing what you love is your only purpose.

Give yourself permission to do what you love. In fact, consider it your first priority. You will find time opening up in your life, as if you opened the dam of an infinitely supplied river, only yours will be a river of time. Giving yourself permission to do what you love takes an awful lot of reprogramming for the average person (a category that includes all of us). We have all been given the idea that the right thing to do is to be safe and practical and, above all else, to avoid failure. We have also been given the idea that putting ourselves first is something we should avoid like the plague.

Obviously, if you can put anything into action, by all means do it—and don't be afraid to make a mistake; this is all part of the learning process. If you are blessed to know what you want to do, then do it; if you are equally blessed to know what you don't want to do, then don't do those activities. Go see a movie, get a massage, go dancing, or visit a museum full of art if you love it. If you don't, then don't go see a movie, dance, get a massage, or go to a museum. Make plans with a friend just to enjoy his or her company. Cancel plans with a friend when you don't feel like going. Be selfish.

In fact, you can't get to your goal of living with unlimited time, or heaven on earth, without making "mistakes." I put that word in quotation marks because it is a misnomer. Even when you believe you have made a mistake—even a simple one, like turning down the wrong street—there is a purpose to it. If you keep your eyes and ears open, you may meet someone who has a key to get you where you want to go more quickly and with less effort. If you feel drawn to the "wrong" person in a relationship, understand that that person can be your greatest teacher, if you just open your eyes. In the end—and it may take a few relationships—if you take responsibility for your experiences, you will share your life with someone who truly inspires you and loves you—instead of tolerating someone who tolerates you.

If you are in a relationship that isn't everything you want, time will be constricted. You have to spend time going through the motions and finding out what the acceptable motions are. On the other hand, when you are in a passionate and supportive relationship, the actions flow without attention or thought. Time expands when love is in the air. Time expands when you are passionate about the moment and the people and activities in that moment.

In the day-to-day observation of what makes you tick, try limiting what you do to what attracts you, what you are passionate about, and what gives you joy. To the best of your ability, only spend time with people you enjoy or are attracted to. To the best of your ability, only do what inspires you. This will seem like a monumental task as you have, up until now, thought that being selfish is a "bad" thing that should be beaten out of you.

Many of us fear disapproval so very much that the thought of being selfish causes us stress. It is true that when you do what you want to do, there will be people in your life who will disapprove of you. When you think logically about the situation, though, you will have to admit that doing what you are supposed to do and catering to the idea of not being "selfish" does not protect you from disapproval. You can't please all people, so why not do what you are supposed to do and please yourself? Either way, you will find disapproval until you approve of yourself. If you are waiting to get approval from outside of yourself, it will never come; you must give it to yourself first.

If you are a person who is not drawn to anything or any person, well, we have other work to do. This may be the root of the entire issue of not having time for you. You are very hard on yourself or very hard on others—or both. You also may be so fearful of who you really are that you are not even conscious of that fact. The real you will be fluid with desire, passion, and inspiration. The real you will want to go places, do things, and meet people—or have absolute knowledge that you don't and peace with that knowledge. If you find your greatest joy in solitude, going nowhere, and doing nothing—then do it. That is what you need to do right now. It may change later, but we are addressing the selfish choice of the now. The majority of us will find that there is a balance between action and inaction, and that balance will be different for each one of us.

Say, for example, that you are have no desire to do anything and want to sit quietly without interruption. If you force yourself to do something, you may get a sense of fleeting approval from yourself for "accomplishing"—but you will end up needing this fleeting sense of accomplishment for your well-being and become addicted to it. That is a much better addiction than heroin, perhaps, in the small picture. In the big picture, though, as your eternal being goes, you can spend your whole life accomplishing things and die without ever having lived your purpose, which is to love, enjoy, and experience what you desire.

On the other hand, you may decide to sit and, while you sit, you have an inspiring revelation, which leads to spending the rest of your life having joyful experiences, and leading others, by your example, to be joyful—and there is world peace and the end of hunger. It could happen. Maybe you sit quietly and become more depressed. In the clutches of depression, you become a heroin addict and end up losing everything you have. In the depth of despair, you look deeply into yourself and recognize your truth, triumphing over your loss and rebuilding a joyful life where you inspire others to their fullest potential—and then there is world peace and the end of hunger. I am, of course, making all of this up, but there are examples of all of this in the lives of many. I certainly am not recommending that you get depressed, become a heroin addict, and lose all of your worldly possessions, your health, and your relationships in order to be all that you can be. I am recommending that you avoid the life of quiet desperation, spent living someone else's idea of a perfect life, in order to be safe. It is actually not safe anyway.

I am not trying to diminish the typical or accepted lifestyle in your present microcosm, as there are many who do it joyfully and who are living exactly the way they are inspired to be. I am trying to show you that all ways can be right or wrong, and the only way you know if a path is right for you is the feeling of joy and passion when you follow it. Only you know whether this is so when you are attending that PTA meeting or not.

Even if you don't yet know what it is you want to do with your life or what you are passionate about, you can begin making more time to figure it out by eliminating unnecessary activities. Remember—it is your first priority to do what you love. You owe it to yourself and humanity; it is your mission. If you are able to bring yourself to cut out some activities, don't waste another minute; cut out the activity. Don't volunteer for any new obligations or take on new activities unless you give it a day or two of serious consideration. When you are asked to do something, even something as simple as giving someone a ride that will take ten minutes, remember that everything takes longer than it is supposed to, and it will stop the flow of your day. At first, you will have to get very "selfish" with your time. You may even want to make it a point to say no to everything new unless you are passionately interested in it; at the very least, get in the habit of "checking your schedule" before you say yes to any request. Obviously, if you had all the time in the world, you could be spontaneous, but you wouldn't be reading this if you had all the time in the world. We are going to get you to that place where you do and then you can be spontaneous, and every spontaneous activity, even giving someone a ride, will be an adventure that enhances your life. Until then, you are going to have to be very picky about what you give your life to. This is a temporary state, meant to get you to the place where you have plenty of time on your hands, even when you are doing everything you want to do. You can then take advantage of the gifts the universe sends your way, moment by moment.

Remember, though, even while you are being strict and selfish with your time—if you feel especially drawn to an activity, and I mean it draws you by your heart and soul and body and mind, then by all means go with it, even if you don't have any "extra time." The universe always makes time for your passions if you follow them. You are only being strict in order to rid yourself of all the distracters you have filled your life with thus far, not to keep you from your purpose. Your purpose will give you joy and passion beyond your wildest imaginings, and it will help in this time crunch you think you have.

While you are checking your schedule, you might also want to check out your motivation for doing whatever it is that you have scheduled. Do you feel obligated to do it? If you feel obligated, then why? Do you think that people will think less of you if you say no? Do you think you may lose a promotion? Do you feel that your children won't think that you love them or that they will suffer some handicap in life? Do you have the idea that it won't get done properly if you don't do it? You may not believe this, but anything done out of fear and without passion does not serve you, your children, or the rest of humanity, even if it is the "right" thing to do. Try your best to let go of those things that you are not passionate about. It will be difficult to do this in the beginning, and you may have to start with small things. You may only be able to give up checking your children's homework once or twice a week before you can give it up completely, for example. Not checking your children's homework might go against what you believe that a responsible parent should do, and I am not saying that this approach is for every parent or for every child—but it is an option. I let my children be responsible for their actions—or their inaction. If they need my help, I am there, but if they miss a homework assignment, they are responsible for the consequences.

Other ways to clear your schedule? You may miss a meeting or resign from a club that is not giving you joy. You could let the house stay cluttered for a day, or hire a cleaning person instead of doing it yourself. Don't plant flowers this year, or hire a lawn service as often as you can afford it. Take a television holiday—you may be surprised at how much time you spend watching fictional people live their lives.

On the other hand, don't be afraid to jump into that which inspires you. Inspirational activities add time to your day and your life. When you jump into an inspirational activity, don't get dragged into the parts of that activity that may *not* inspire you. For example, if you join a singing group, and they happen to be looking for someone to coordinate the practice sessions or host the group, but this is not your cup of tea, then do not volunteer for that aspect. Someone will come to the table, or the group will find a way to divide up the duties.

Any activities that you do because you would feel guilty not doing them should be the first to go. There are plenty of people in the world who will continue to do these things for the right and wrong reasons. If enough people stop doing needless activities that accomplish nothing or, at best, are inefficient, things will change. If we continue to support wasteful, "obligatory" activities, they will prosper like the weeds they are in the lawn of life. It is very clear that there are a few people who carry the weight of any endeavor no matter how many people are involved. They are either motivated by passion or fear.

You cannot be the judge of someone else's motivation or responsible for another person's life, but you can make sure that you are not the person motivated by fear or guilt. If you are the person motivated by fear or guilt, you may not have the ability to stop right away. For now, it is enough to be aware. You will get to the place where you are no longer motivated by fear.

Don't waste your time on activities because it looks good on your resume of life. If you are that person and not motivated by passion, it's time to realize that, if you stop doing what you are doing, someone else will pick up the ball—or the activity has reached its final resting place. There is no ritual, activity, club, or tradition that will last forever; at some point, everything has to either end or change. Be daring and let natural selection work in the game of life. Just because a society or club or group has been around for thirty or a hundred years doesn't mean it has to be around for one more day. Even if the group is doing "good things" for the community, the void will be filled with something equal or better.

Anything done out of fear, which is another way of classifying obligation, ought to be stopped as well, if you can get over your fear. Getting over your fear means that you have to recognize what the fear is and get rid of the belief that causes the fear.

A common motivation for parents is a fear of failure on behalf of their children. We try so hard to protect our children from the failure we fear that we end up setting them up for failure—or, even worse, pushing them into living their lives as we live ours.

Are you happy with your life right at this moment? Or are you waiting for it to get better? We pound into our children that they have to "work hard" and do something practical with their lives, but we do not give them the courage to do what they love. Even more damaging—we give them the example of a life not fulfilled, a life that is stressed and crammed full of activity we are not truly interested in. We give them the example of just following the crowd and being "safe." We give them the example of believing other people's opinions instead of our own. Unfortunately, they will follow our example most of the time.

Don't you want your children to be happy, to make their dreams come true, to be independent of other people's opinions so they will always feel good about themselves? In truth, encouraging them to live this way is the safest thing to do for them. You might as well be happy so that you can handle the exciting challenges of life instead of being stressed and unfulfilled. When you feel stressed and unfulfilled, the challenges of life become burdens and problems instead of adventures and challenges. Tomorrow, everything in your life could change. Nothing is stable or for sure, so let go of the illusion you cling to, that you are safe living this compromised life, doing what everyone else does and doing what you are "supposed to" do. If you knew you were going to die soon, how would you change your life? Well, guess what, we are all going to die soon; life is short, no matter how long you live, and none of us gets out alive. It sounds morbid to say that. Another way to look at it, though, is that you are an eternal being and the real you never dies. Getting over the fear of moving into the next experience, the one called death, is important. Live like there is no tomorrow and also like you are eternal.

Realizing that the world will go on without you makes it possible to step off and take a breather. Try to get rid of everything that is not absolutely necessary. For example, stop baking cookies for bake sales; buy them instead if you must get involved—unless, of course, you are truly passionate about baking cookies. I am going to say something radical here, but doing things just to accomplish something is avoiding your purpose. We have been trained as children and positively reinforced to think that this avoidance behavior is a virtue. It is not. That doesn't make it a bad thing, just an avoidance behavior to be recognized for what it is. If you must accomplish things, that implies that you are in need of approval and still dependent on others for your true identity and purpose. When you release the need to accomplish things and your dependence on the external feedback you get from the accomplishment, you will be able to truly see if the things you do really suit your purpose.

This does not mean accomplishment is a bad thing; it is neither good nor bad. I am also not saying that you should become someone who does nothing. On the contrary—you will accomplish more once you become detached from the need to accomplish, and it will be what you were meant to do. It will be easy, though it seems to all who observe you that you are doing incredible things, and it will be done in minimal time with the least amount of effort. The effort will be like playing your favorite game, and that is because it will be your favorite game. It is not that you should stop doing or accomplishing, but that you must get in touch with your motivation. You will find that, when you are in touch with what you truly want to do, you will have plenty of time to do it. When you are not in touch with what you truly want to do or afraid of doing it, you fill your life with excuses for not doing it or find yourself in a wild goose chase for completion that can never be attained.

In order to do what you are passionate about, avoid confusing that with the things you "find" a way to enjoy or things you don't mind doing. We tend to fill our lives with tolerable activities because, deep down, we fear doing the thing we love the most. That also leaves us with the illusion of having no time left and gives us the excuse to avoid our truth. When you think about it, if you had enough time to do it all, then you would have no excuse for the fears that you may wrestle with. Let's say you are really passionate about playing the piano. When you play, you are in another world, filled with joy. There is no accomplishment, however, so you put off your playing in favor of doing all of the things you feel obligated to do. You do all the things that will get you approval from society or your family, whichever you find holds your power. You may also find that you accomplish things to avoid disapproval from those same people. Realize that you have given them power over you, and take it back. Realize also that when you take it back, those who had the power will try to stop you, so it may be difficult at first. Just as children will scream all the louder when they know they have a chance at getting what they want, they will also stop when they realize it isn't working.

It is the same with those who would have power over you. At first, they will pull out all the stops to keep you in line, and when they finally know you are set on your path, they will stop trying to control you. They are equally frightened of someone who tries to change their world, so don't be angry. Instead, have compassion for them, if you can. Of course, that means you have to actually believe that what you are doing is right, believe in yourself, and have no fear of change. Know also that when you seek and live your grandest vision of yourself, you help open everyone else around you to that potential.

Sometimes it may seem that you are "hurting" someone by doing your thing, but in fact, you are doing him or her a favor. After you have detached yourself from someone who has a vested interest in controlling you, it is up to that person to make the best of the situation or find someone else to continue the power struggle with. It is also true that, if someone has been controlling you, you have allowed it and are equally responsible. Many times, we allow someone to control us because it is "easier" and gives us someone else to blame when we "fall short" or are not happy with the circumstances of our lives. Do not feel as if these people have taken advantage of you; you are equally responsible for the interaction.

How many times have we used the excuse that we can't do something because someone in our life will be angry if we do it? We actually can do whatever we want, regardless of anyone else's attempt to control us. I personally used this excuse in the past and blamed my spouse for not being able to engage in activities I loved, saying that he would be angry. I realized that his anger could not affect me unless I chose to be affected. When I chose to not be affected, he stopped being angry. It is amazing how that happens—but it does. When in your heart of hearts you are no longer attached to approval and the opinions of others, you will find that everyone in your world supports you.

If you do not engage yourself in passionate activities, you will find yourself feeling like something is missing or that you are not "doing" enough or that you are less than others in some way. On the other hand, when you are passionate, you connect with your divine nature and have a sense of peace. Now, you may wonder how that will give you more time in your life, and in this, you will have to trust me. Being at peace with yourself and others draws into your life the balance that you seek. The people who you come in contact with will have more peace and function more efficiently; you will also function more efficiently. You will be stimulating your immune system and the immune systems of those around you, so you will have more energy and be healthier. You will find the motivation you have been missing. You will naturally need less sleep. These are well-documented findings relating to the relaxation response studied by doctors and scientists over the years and published by medical, psychology, and scientific journals. You will be less addicted to the opinions of other people and, ironically, you may find their opinions more to your liking when they are presented to you. The world around you is a direct reflection of your inner thoughts and beliefs.

If you realized how magnificent a being you are, you would not have to continue to prove it to yourself. In so doing, you will provide yourself with unlimited time to do what you want to do, are joyful doing, and are inspired to do. In so doing, you actually do more for world peace than if you spend your life in war-torn areas taking care of people. Unless, of course, you are there because it gives you incredible joy and you are passionate about it. People who do that kind of thing are usually motivated properly, as it would be difficult to spend time in those areas unless you were inspired, but no one person can know another's motivation. Often we judge them to be superior beings and then feel ourselves to be less than magnificent. We are all equally magnificent, no matter what we do, even if we do waste moments in quiet desperation.

The people you spend your time with and choose to live with can also encroach on your time if you are pretending to love, doing what is expected, instead of truly loving. Filling your life with love of self and people who truly love you and whom you truly love will create more time in your life in a number of ways.

When you truly love someone and you truly love yourself, you give others the freedom to be and do, instead of trying to mold them into what you want, which takes an incredible amount of time and energy. When you are with those who truly love you, they give you that same freedom, and you have no need to get involved in activities in order to prove your love.

Let go of doing things because you are supposed to do them. Instead, do what you are inspired to do by love in each moment. I promise it will all work out. Love yourself first, unconditionally, and watch how magically your life is filled with people who love you that way. This will free you to do only what you want to do, inspired by love, with those you love and who love you.

You probably remember times when you were engaged in an activity with your friends or your lover or both and time was not an issue. You had so much fun and enjoyed whatever it was you were doing. I will bet it has been a long time since you could just be in that moment and enjoy life without worry, guilt, or preoccupation with some thing you "had to get done." You may even think that those moments are for the young and newly in love. That is so far from the truth! Living in that kind of joy can be your everyday life, if you will allow it.

Get selfish for the sake of all humanity. Get selfish for the sake of finding time. Get selfish for the sake of your true purpose. Get selfish because you can only give something of true value to another when you are madly in love with yourself and doing what you are passionate about.

Chapter Five

Change Beliefs That
Don't Serve You

We have bought into the idea that only a few people do what they love and they are lucky. Luck has nothing to do with it. We have also fallen into the idea that life requires hard work and enjoyment is the exception to the rule. All of these concepts will be true if you continue to believe they are true. What you believe becomes your reality, and, until you change what you think and believe differently, you will never have enough time.

Change your mind if you want your life to be different, but be aware that it will become different—can you handle the wonderment of heaven on earth? Are you ready for change? Everything will change. If this makes you uncomfortable, then you will need to work on your fears before you can make time work for you. You cannot make changes in your life if you are afraid of them; it just won't happen. Having enough time to do what you want will absolutely change your life, so in order to have enough time you have to get rid of your fear of change. Do you follow?

The fear of change works against you. Because change will happen anyway, you might as well get over your fear and be the one who directs the change in your life. Sometimes all it takes is for someone to point out how illogical a belief really is. I am pointing out to you that fearing change is illogical. It is like fearing a new day. It is going to happen, and you signed up for it—so why fear it?

Changing your beliefs is a process of bringing into your awareness those beliefs that work against you, causing you to create a suboptimal life where you have no time to do what you were born to do and experience. To change your mind, be vigilant about your thoughts, especially the subtle, almost unheard, ones that keep telling you to feel guilty for having a good time or that are telling you that hard work will get you what you want.

Realize that, to everyone else, a person immersed in what he or she loves will appear to be working long and hard when, in reality, that person is having an incredibly blissful experience. People are always telling me that I work hard—and I tell them that I never work. Each time your mind comes at you with a belief you no longer want, change the thought to what you do want to believe, and repeat it to yourself as often as you need to hear it. It can be as simple as, "It is my purpose to do what I love and enjoy my life." This appears to be selfish, but it has been my experience that those most happy with their lives do more for the world and for other people than those who are not happy with their lives.

Again, sometimes it is as simple as opening your eyes and looking at what is really going on in life. We are blessed and cursed with so much information about the world and what goes on in it. It is clear that there is no rhyme or reason to anything. The only logical conclusion is that we are all creating our reality with our amazing and powerful thoughts. The proof will be in your experience, once you start changing your chronic thought patterns by exposing them to the light.

There are so many ways to eliminate beliefs that don't serve you. I found that what worked for me was to use every negative feeling that I had as a trigger to look within and see what belief was there that didn't serve me. I could wake up in the morning and immediately be worried about something. It could be anything from not having something the kids needed for school to feeling a weird ache in my ankle and wondering what could be causing it, to having to deal with a difficult case at work. It could be any number of things. As soon as I accepted that the negative feeling or "worry" was a result of my thoughts and beliefs that were in error, I found relief. I didn't even have to eradicate the belief. Simply knowing that I could and that my feelings were in my power to change made a difference.

When you are experiencing a negative emotion, just changing your focus from what you think is causing the emotion to focusing on what inside of you is allowing that emotion puts you in the adventure-and-discovery mode. Now you are the detective, going within to find the source of your feeling—not the person feeling it.

Most of the beliefs that cause us to be fearful or worried or guilt-ridden are there because we haven't accepted the truth about ourselves. We are magnificent, spectacular, and unlimited beings having a temporary time-space experience. To get rid of any and all negative emotions, we have to own that truth—and own it for everyone else as well. Lighten up on yourself and others, and continue the adventure within that explores why you are living less than your dream life, where you would have all the time in the world.

Some would argue that I am not in touch with reality, but reality is so different for each one of us. My original idea was that I would just change how I thought, just so that I could feel better in each moment. I was not even aware of my part in creating the reality that I lived. I just knew that I didn't have enough time and felt like life was a constant struggle. I started thinking differently, just to feel better, and I noticed that my circumstances were changing. Events in my life were changing. People in my life were changing. In addition, I was getting more done in less time and not rushing or struggling to do it. I found that I was actually the creator of all my circumstances—by experience. I would suggest that you do the same.

If you don't have enough time, then realize that you have created that fact with your constant thoughts about time—and change how you think about time. The best way to expand time is to be relaxed and completely present in the moment. Unless you are choosing to enjoy a memory or to enjoy a future anticipated event, be with the task at hand and the people who are showing up now.

The belief that you must dig up negative past events and guard against them for the future actually increases the odds that you will experience those negative events again. Change the belief; realize that the negative event was created by a different you. It served to help you clarify what it is you *do* want in life and to envision how you want it to be.

The belief that you have no control of circumstances is another one to get rid of. The idea that you have no control of circumstances is distasteful, so why keep it? You are, by now, at least entertaining the idea that you create your world. If so, you might as well believe only what makes you feel the best. The problem with believing that you create your experiences is that you can't blame anyone else anymore. It is a small price to pay to have your life back. Take responsibility without blaming yourself either. Think of yourself as someone who is just learning a new skill, and be patient.

If someone is keeping you waiting or "wasting" your time, take responsibility and use that time for a great thought, a future vision, a gratitude moment, or whatever your mind can do that makes you feel good. Then the time is not actually wasted, and you will find that it opens up time for you in the future. It opens up people and events who facilitate your dreams. What is the point of having plenty of time if you aren't living your dream life?

There are other ways to eliminate beliefs that don't serve you, and most techniques are aimed at getting your attention off the belief that doesn't serve you and replacing that belief with one that does serve you. NLP (neurolinguistic programming), guided imagery, self-hypnosis, hypnosis, and EFT (emotional freedom technique) are just a few options. Information about most of these can be found on YouTube for free, and you can certainly spend anywhere from a dollar to thousands on replacing your beliefs with more life-giving beliefs.

Chapter Six

The Illusion of Busy

People often get caught up in the illusion that they can get more than one thing done at a time. You can only do one thing, in one place, at any one time. Even when you think you are multitasking, all you are doing is cutting multiple activities up into little pieces and mixing them together. If you argue that you can eat and drive at the same time, thus accomplishing two things at once, I will tell you that whatever you ate will not count as far as your body is concerned, and you will feel that you need to eat again to nourish yourself. This will add to your net weight and thus add stress to your life, not to mention heartburn and possible car accidents. You are still only accomplishing one thing at a time. If you stay focused on the task you are doing at the moment, you will not feel stressed. Don't think about the last task or the task to come; give the one you are doing now your full attention, and you will be relaxed. This will accomplish two things: you will be more efficient and time will actually expand. I have seen it happen in my own practice.

I decided to stop worrying about running late and to give my full attention to each patient and also to take as much time as my patients needed to have all of their questions answered and fears addressed. It seems miraculous, but now I get out on time virtually every day, where I used to run late routinely. I am still amazed by this phenomenon. When you start feeling stressed by the pressures of your day, say to yourself, "I can only do one thing at one time in one place." You can't be any busier than that, no matter how hard you try, and no matter what someone else wants you to do. Just bringing this fact into your awareness can release the pressure, because you cannot change this fact; it is a phenomenon of human existence. In fact, from your broader eternal perspective, that is how you set up your physical world. Feeling stress over something you cannot change is a waste of your life force; it suppresses your immune system and robs you of your time.

Giving the task at hand your undivided attention and not letting yourself obsess over something that just happened, how well you did it, or what someone thought of you is a key ingredient. Not letting yourself get caught up in thinking ahead to what you have to do next or whether you are running late or how much more you have to do or anticipating someone's negative reaction is also important. There is a time and place for looking at the past and preparing for the future, but you should be the one to take yourself to those places when you choose. You should not have to engage in a constant struggle with your mind over focusing on a past event or anticipating a future circumstance; when you choose to be involved in the present moment, this is where you should be.

You will find that if you give people your undivided attention, they will overlook almost anything. People in general are starving for attention, which is the love they seek outside themselves. The irony is that the love they seek is actually inside of them, not outside. Even so, giving someone your undivided attention is very attractive to that person. He or she will be drawn to you and tend to think highly of you. When someone enjoys your company and is genuinely interested in you, it is natural for you to want to like that person. This works the other way as well: you will soon find yourself attracting what and whom you need in your life.

Be aware that this can also backfire. If you allow yourself to become the life force for a particular individual or find yourself tempted to use this talent as a way to control others, it will start to detract from your life. In fact, you may find that this is already the case. People generally have a combination of arrangements in their lives. In most cases, they are unaware of the reasons behind all of their interactions and relationships. Life becomes a roller coaster of emotions that can't be predicted or prepared for. In one relationship, you are controlling; in another, someone is controlling you. In one, you are giving, and in another, you are taking. Even those who believe they are the ultimate doormats, being used and giving of themselves constantly, are often using passive aggression to control others.

If you are running late or something is not going right for you in a situation, come into the interaction with the absolute conviction that this is the way it was meant to be for some grand purpose. Your attitude will change, and the change will affect everything and everyone for the better. Being stuck in traffic can be transformed into your life being saved, or an accident being prevented. It becomes a time for you to commune with the divine, see beautiful pictures in nature, or listen to amazing music. When something slows me down, I take the hint and look around. If you don't make it to an appointment, then it wasn't meant to be. That doesn't mean that you don't need to assess how you plan your days or how sincerely you were motivated to get there. It does mean that you weren't meant to get there today for some grand purpose in your life. Life will always work out to your benefit if you are aware, have your internal eyes open, and have enough love for yourself to look honestly at all of the messages being sent your way.

Whenever you are faced with something that is not going the way you planned, or life is not going "your way," look for the message in this blessed event. If you stay stuck on complaining about it or feeling like it is outside your control, or you believe that someone else is to blame, you will never see the truth. The pattern will repeat until you change the way you see it. Some people live their whole lives this way, and the joy of living eludes them. You may be one of those people, constantly saying that nothing goes the way you want it to or the way you plan in your life. There will come a time when you celebrate that your life hasn't gone as you planned, because it is so much better than you imagined.

Chapter Seven

Think Highly of Others

Trusting other people and thinking highly of others gives you more time in two ways: It allows you to delegate tasks in your life and work more freely. It also brings out the best in the people who work around and for you. You will find people doing more than you asked for, going the extra mile for you. You will attract people who are doing what they love in their life, complementing your ability to do what you love in your life. Like puzzle pieces fitting together, things will finally seem to come together. Can you handle a great life like that, or does it make you uneasy? I repeat, you must get in touch with your fear of success. You don't have to do or be anything to deserve success. Success is your birthright.

I have a friend who was complaining about all the incompetent people in his life and work. I asked him if he could handle a world where people were competent and did their jobs incredibly well. He had to stop and think—he truly couldn't answer the question. How would you feel if you had nothing to complain about? Would you feel good about yourself if everyone else were wonderful and beautiful and competent? How would you rate yourself if there were no one to be better than? A key ingredient to successful time management is to adore yourself without a relative standard. This means that your worth is

God-given, and you are spectacular no matter what you have done, are doing, or haven't done. It means that you are fabulous and equal to all the other fabulous spirits in human form.

In my own life, as I released attachments to old, worn-out ideas like "you have to work hard to justify help with household chores" and "the only way to be a good and loving mother is to do laundry, cook, and clean," I found myself attracting the means and the people in my life to get those things done for me. Ironically, this has allowed me to love my children even more fully and to work less. I also found that, in every aspect of my work and personal life, the people around me became more efficient the more I thought highly of them. I didn't have to say anything or encourage them; simply changing the way I thought made the difference. This obviously provides me with more time to do what I love, so, in turn, I become more efficient and productive. Thinking highly of others is easy, much easier than finding fault with them.

We waste a lot of time protecting ourselves from being taken advantage of, but, for the most part, people are not out to take advantage of you. In fact, if you look at yourself closely, you are probably apt to give more than you receive. You are more likely to give yourself the short stick than give it to someone else. I find this is true for most people. So why do we assume that the rest of the world is so different and that we are the only giving and just people? I am not recommending a complete lack of caution. I am saying that you might want to rethink your beliefs about others. What is so bad about being taken advantage of, anyway? For the most part, you aren't losing anything of great worth. I personally don't give it a second thought. I choose to believe that if anyone thinks that he or she has taken advantage of me, that person will be blessed by the result of that interaction and his or her life will become beautiful and change that person for the better, and the world will benefit. Call me crazy, but there is nothing I have that is so important to me that I have to waste time protecting it. I am finding that the universe supports my belief; in fact, it supports any belief, good or bad, so I choose to believe that which makes me happiest.

Believing in the good of others brings out the good in others. This will give you time to do what you love instead of wasting it on protection from things that aren't even going to happen. I am not saying this is for everyone, but it works for me. For example, I don't have to consult with lawyers often, because contracts are fair, and I trust the people I deal with. Another example is that when I contract for work to be done, I don't have to get five different bids, because whoever I happen to be dealing with is fair and competent. You can say that I will never know for sure, but I am the one who has all the time in the world to do what I love and then some. For the last five years, I have gotten more out of life financially, personally, physically, and emotionally than in all my previous years. In addition, I seem to work less. In fact, I feel like I am on vacation every day. I trust my instincts and intuition, and they don't fail me. If a little voice says *don't go there,* I try not to go there. If it says that it is okay to proceed, then I proceed. If it says I should lock my car door, then I do—but normally, I don't lock anything up. It isn't a little voice really, just a feeling, and I try to be in touch with how I am feeling.

I am not wantonly irresponsible, and I do look at things I do with intelligence and clear sight. An example is the trust people put in me to do their surgery. There is no way for a person to gain the amount of education and experience I have in one visit or the few weeks or months before I do the surgery. They have to trust me, and the more they trust me, the better they will do. It works like that in all walks of life. Someone could research roofing companies for months and then pick one—and have the same results he or she would have gotten by just using the first name that came up in the phone book. Each of us should do it the way we "believe" it should be done. What is the worst thing that can happen? The roof leaks, or you lose money or some *thing* You see, to me, none of that is worth my valuable time— time that I spend loving people and life and experiences. The ironic thing is that, when you put your priorities in order, life has a way of handling the details. This, of course, frees up more time. Yes, I have been called crazy, but again, I remind you that I am the one living heaven on earth, being gloriously happy, and enjoying uncanny "good luck." So I ask you, to whom are you going to pay attention—me or all of those neurotic and unhappy people who are worried about being taken advantage of?

Chapter Eight

Making the Most of Now

If you believe you can't change your situation, then you will not be able to change your situation. Start telling yourself that you can change it—even if at first you don't know how. Just opening your mind to the possibility will bring solutions. In the meantime, make the most of what you are doing. If you are involved with people, talk to them. See what they are about and what ideas they have. If you are engaged in an activity, look around to see if there is a way to make it more fun. Look into ways your work can educate you. Think outside the box, and keep your awareness active. This way, you can find your blocks to happiness. These are the real reasons you can't change your life. It has nothing to do with the lot life dealt you and everything to do with what you believe and the choices you continue to make. These are mostly choices about what you believe, not about what you do. What you believe leads ultimately to what you do, but when you have great beliefs, what you do is easy and fun. You can believe differently and make different choices, starting today.

There is a lovely story about three bricklayers and their attitudes about their work. The first felt that he was just working, putting his time in. The second felt that he was constructing a beautiful building. The third felt that he was creating a sacred place for people to experience their connection with the divine. Can you imagine how wonderful work would seem if you felt such inspiration and grand purpose? You see, you can re-create your existence with just a change of thought. Making the most of a situation does not imprison you in the situation; instead, it puts you in a position where you can spring into your heart's desire. I will repeat— making the most of a situation, finding whatever good you can in it, does not mean you learn to live with it. It is actually the best way to improve or change it to what you really want.

Whatever situation you are in has a purpose for you, and if you uncover its purpose, you will be ready to move into the next place, a place that will be closer and closer to your heart's desire. The fact that you are where you are, doing what you are doing in this moment, is the proof that, in this moment, it is what you must be doing and it is where your purpose is. That doesn't mean that, in the next minute, you can't create your dream life. (Of course, you must have some idea what that dream life is and be willing to allow it.)

How does this give you more time in your life? It expands time, thus creating more time in your life. Sounds funny, but keep your mind open, and your experience will be the proof. In bringing inspiration to your present day, you start attracting time expansion. In miraculous ways, when you work with inspiration and love, you are in the moment, and it seems that time slows down to accommodate your work. It also makes you more efficient and creative, so you seem to benefit in two ways. In fact, you also benefit from an increase in *quality* of time. You actually start realizing how much fun your life is and how much fun you and people around you are. You laugh more and live more of your moments in joy.

Just as an aside, the issue of having more time is really not about having more time but about experiencing more joy, love, and fun in each and every moment. If you were experiencing that in every moment of your life, you would not feel an issue of time.

Thinking outside the box is another consideration. For example, if you find yourself having to make your kids do chores, and it becomes more time consuming to nag them to do it, remind them multiple times, and then the job's still only half-done—stop making your kids do chores. It is not written in any rulebook that children must do chores or that doing so will make them better people. Hire a neighbor's child to do the same thing. It will be relatively cheap, and he or she will do a great job. Your children would do a great job for your neighbor, wouldn't they? Do not demean your children; just say it is business, and you do not have time to nag and would prefer to spend more quality time with them. Your children might actually want the job; if so, they will then do it responsibly.

So here you are, thinking that it may be possible to avoid doing things that you don't want to do and only to do what gives you joy. Treat others as if that were true—including your children. You want them to blossom in life, not end up in the same prison you are trying to escape.

If you don't like to cook but don't mind doing laundry, try connecting with someone who feels the opposite way. You can work out a way to exchange services. If you can afford to have someone do some of your chores, don't hesitate to hire someone. You will not be less for having done so, even if you just "waste" the time you gain. The universe abhors a vacuum and will fill your time with what you want—provided you have given yourself permission to be happy and do what you love, guilt-free.

If you can't see how to change a certain situation this red-hot minute, then find a way to make it fun. Use the creative genius you have. For example, on a long "unwanted" commute, listen to motivational audio programs. This makes use of the time in a way that will free you from your limiting beliefs. Or listen to inspiring music or dictate your memoirs onto a hands-free recording device. Practice singing or do car exercises or call people and reconnect. Do whatever will take your mind away from being unhappy with the commute. It is a strange yet universal phenomenon that as soon as you make peace with the situation you hate, it is soon to leave you.

Let's say that you usually do laundry and housecleaning on the weekend, but you have managed to get someone to do that in exchange for making a few dinners that you freeze and deliver. You make these for your family anyway, so you can just double the amount. Then, when your exchange buddy sends her cleaning lady to your house, grateful for your home cooking and finding someone to do it, you sit there, not knowing what to do with yourself. This will not last—soon you will make plans to meet with friends, take a class, or get a massage. You will enjoy just being quiet or reading a book. It will feel like you are on vacation, and new experiences and possibilities will open up because you are connecting to your inner self and others. When you open your experience to other possibilities, the universe steps in and gives you what you want. It has been waiting to step in and deliver, but you were too busy making yourself unavailable.

Housework or yard work can be unnecessary drains on your time, unless you are passionate about doing them. Again, it is very simple to cut down or delegate these tasks. A big part of making this happen is to realize that your self-worth is not dependent on the act of cleaning or creating a great lawn. This is not to say that you don't want a clean house or beautiful lawn. A cleaning service will cost you a night out to dinner, a half day of work, an outfit. Hire one once a year or once a month, whatever you can afford. Hire neighbor children, barter with your kids for transportation services, and barter with your friends. Brainstorm about how you can get the job done without doing it yourself. Trade doing activities you don't like for ones you do. Ask for gifts of professional cleaning services from your family for special occasions. Lower your standards for a while. Just becoming open to the possibility of finding the right help will start bringing the opportunities to you. If it seems too hard to arrange, then you still have some inner resistance. It works like magic when you are not resistant. I repeat, if it seems difficult, then you have resistance. It will work like magic when the resistance is gone.

I had a very difficult time finding a reliable babysitter to watch my kids after school, and I found no cleaning people who did a great job—until I stopped believing that only the mother should be doing this work. When I released that worn-out belief, I found cleaning people who were amazing. Then, when I was pregnant with my youngest and needed a full-time sitter, one of the cleaning women asked me for the job. She literally fell into my lap, and she not only watched my children, she did everything but cook dinner for me. She is one of my best friends and has made life for me a blessing. Imagine coming home to a perfectly immaculate house, laundry clean, beds made, groceries bought and put away, dry cleaning picked up, and your small child clean, happy, and with perfect hair. She is truly a magical woman who just happened into my life.

I have learned from men that if you ignore a job long enough, someone steps up to the plate to do it—usually a woman (he he). If you pay attention, it is amazing how people react to a clean or unclean house. If you walk into a man's house and say it is a mess, he will casually agree with you and ignore it. It will not affect his self-worth or make him feel badly. Say the same thing to a woman, and she will have an emotional reaction—defense, self-loathing, or excuses. She has attached her self-worth to a clean house; he has not. The house belongs to both of them, but they react to this situation differently. What you are attached to controls you. Men have their own attachments to get over, but you can learn much from them in the world of doing things they love. I am just making an observation that women could learn a thing or two from men in following their passions and not being attached to obligations.

Experiment with the principle that if something is left undone long enough, someone will do it. Try not doing things you normally do and see what happens—I bet the world doesn't stop turning, and you may find some tasks actually do get done without you. It is a good exercise in separating your self-worth from what you do. Simply be worthy of all that you desire because you exist. If this makes you uncomfortable, then you have your first clue that you are dependent on your doing. There is nothing wrong with doing; in fact, it is glorious when you are joyful at it. Being dependent on it only serves to take away your joy. It doesn't make you less or more, as your magnificence is already established—you just have to own it and let it out.

You can start out slowly, with just one thing you don't want to do, and give yourself a comfortable time limit. If you end up doing it in the end and it makes your life more difficult, then the experiment shows that you need to take another approach. This also shows how entrenched you are in the need to be needed. Work on your feelings of self-worth and come to the realization that you are truly *not* needed—and that is a very good thing. Being needed is not being loved; don't confuse the two.

Work on having your self-worth attached to nothing. In fact, you will be surprised to find that truly loving yourself means loving the you that does nothing. When you come to that state of mind, you will find everything you do is a joy and everyone in your life truly loves you and you them. Isn't that what having all the time in the world is about?

When life hands you lemons, make lemonade. Every time you are "held up" or waiting in line or stuck in traffic or delayed or waiting for a late relative (child or spouse), realize this is happening because you do not take enough time for yourself. This is the universe's way of giving you more time for you. Make use of it by doing a little meditation, or have an inspiring book ready. Have a grateful attitude for these moments instead of seeing them as a problem.

After a while, start taking time to yourself each day on purpose, and increase the amount as often and as much as you can until you come to a day where you can honestly say you have enough time in every day to do all that you want to do. What the heck, if you can go away for a whole day, whole weekend, whole week alone, do it. I guarantee that you will experience fewer delays, and the delays that do happen will be to your advantage. At this point in your life, you will be able to recognize the advantage and make full use of it. You will also be able to avoid the negative emotions of frustration and anger that only serve to suppress your immune system, age you prematurely, and cause you to miss precious gifts that are being presented to you. The person standing in line in front of you may be the one who has the key to whatever it is you are searching for. He or she may just be someone with a great joke that will give you a good laugh and put you in a good mood. Be grateful for every little gift, and the gifts will only increase in size and frequency.

Chapter Nine

Wonderfully Alone; Not Lonely

Which brings us to the next step. If you don't like who you are and can't spend time with yourself pleasurably, you will always subconsciously be attracting, accepting, and instigating "stuff" to fill your life with. This "stuff" is not your passion. You may even be punishing yourself. I hear people saying often that they have already earned their right to heaven with what they have had to put up with in this lifetime. I hate to say it, but everyone can be in heaven, no matter what they do or don't do. Heaven is a state of mind, a way of being—not a place to go.

Giving yourself the benefit of the doubt, truly forgiving yourself for everything, being extremely lenient with yourself, saying encouraging and positive things to yourself—these habits will make you a person *you* want to be with. Once again, this seems to be in conflict with what you have come to believe about fighting your sluggish, unproductive tendencies. There is not one person who ever existed or exists who is lazy; there are simply people who are not motivated. If you are going to insist on doing things you don't want to do, then you will not be motivated and life will be a constant struggle. You will also find that you are not living while you do those tasks but that you are a zombie on autopilot. If you choose to find your passion, you will find life not only easy but lucrative as well. People who are truly successful don't work hard; they do what they love.

The true measure of success is not what you have or who is with you but how you feel every moment of every day. The irony of life is that if you have external success without this knowledge, you are unhappy and without joy. On the other hand, when you have this insight, you will manifest the external success you desire. This will be different for each individual, and you can't determine it for another—you can only know for yourself whether you have what you want. It is possible to live every moment of your life with joy and love, focused on the wonderment of each moment of life, instead of focusing on what isn't "right" with your life. In so doing, you will create the external success—the money, stuff, career, etc.

Getting inspired and happy with where you are is not about limiting your immediate future and settling for less than your dreams. It is actually the quickest and easiest way to make your dreams come true. When that is the case, you will have enormous amounts of time and no room for stress as you make dream after dream come true. You will find it so easy that you will come up with more dreams and joyfully make them come true. Life will become whatever you want it to be from moment to moment. You will not worry about making a mistake because you will know, without a doubt, that you can change your life to fit your hopes and dreams no matter what. If you find yourself in an experience that no longer gives you joy, in that moment you will find joy in the new and exciting idea that springs from that experience. You will also know that it will be here shortly without paying a price.

Stress is always based in fear of something. The fear of being alone is one that truly keeps people imprisoned in a world of obligation and distraction. Get clear about what your fears are, and you will have conquered more than half the battle. Releasing your fears is very simply changing what you believe about yourself and the world. When you realize that you are connected with everyone else and more than your physical self, then you will also know you are never alone. You can be with anyone you want with only a thought. You also have an army of nonphysical beings around you at all times: inner being, God, divine intelligence, angels—whatever and whomever you want. You are the creator of your experience, and the more you exercise your creativity, the more you will excel and enjoy all of your experiences.

The added benefit is that when you become comfortable with being alone, you will always have the choice of having a physical presence if you want. Just as animals smell fear, people sense lack and need. When people sense that in a person, they will run like the wind—unless they have a counter-need to be needed to feel good. This is why, when you are needy and fearful, you attract people into your life who feed into your need and fear, making it seem that you are justified in your neediness and fearfulness. You will attract people into your world who are also fearful or who are looking for fearful people. This is how you create your reality. Just on the surface, this is true, but it is far more complex and deeper than you know. Researchers interviewed inmates in prison and asked them to watch videos of people walking down the street. The inmates said that they would only attack or rob those with body language that indicated weakness, fear, or submissiveness. That is just the surface—body language—but it signifies something deeper.

Your thoughts have a profound effect on your body language. Even more profound than body language is the energy of thought. You know yourself that when you walk into a room where there has been confrontation or anger or pressure, you feel it before you even become aware of what you are seeing. Energy transfer in that regard has not been explained, but it exists—just as gravity existed before it was understood. Whether you understand it or even believe it exists, it has an effect on you.

The good news is that you can use that information to educate yourself about where you have resistance or limiting beliefs—and change those beliefs. You can actually get to a point where you can disarm and eliminate a negative atmosphere with just your presence. Embrace your magical self, for it is so worth doing.

Chapter Ten

The World as Your Mirror

You are an eternal being with no restrictions except those which you have given yourself. Everyone else is in the same boat. When you come up against someone who appears to be restricting you in some way, it is because you have chosen this restriction on some level and because that person feels restricted as well. People who are truly happy with themselves cannot ever restrict others. Any negativity coming your way is a reflection of your own negativity toward yourself, although it may be magnified. Sometimes, the most intense negativity coming in your direction is your greatest gift, as you may be ready to move past it. At some level, you are calling for this to be recognized, and it is becoming a stronger presence in your life.

If you had no personal investment in the negative concept, you would realize that the negativity is not about you, and you would see the negativity differently. The negative action would be from a person in pain, not truly an attack. Take, for example, a person at work verbally attacking you by calling you incompetent. If this were a two-year-old calling you incompetent, you would not even blink an eye. If the person is someone you did not give power to, you might react only slightly, but if it is someone you have given power to, because of some outdated belief or fear, you are likely to have a strong reaction. Your reaction could be anger, indignation, or self-doubt. You might devote much "time" and energy (distracting thoughts that make you less efficient and peaceful) to justification, explanation, worry or guilt, and anxiety. You may then try to counter this insult with some action or look for experiences that will "fix," or at least dull, the bad feeling. You might also look for people who will support you in your outrage and pain, making the person responsible the bad guy.

Sometimes, as with the body, a greater pain will outweigh a lesser pain, and we choose a greater obstacle to diminish the lesser. You may attract another problem that seems out of your control to excuse and distract yourself from the insult. This seems counterproductive and more like cutting off your nose to spite your face. It is not hard to see much of this behavior around you; it is only difficult to see it in yourself.

The miraculous thing about recognizing it in yourself is that, when you start seeing this clearly, the negativity stops coming your way. It truly happens that way. Every time you experience something that leaves you feeling anything but joy and love, look inside yourself for a place where you don't love yourself unconditionally.

The world is truly a mirror, reflecting the sum of your thoughts—without exception. If you are seeing and experiencing things that you don't want, such as feeling that you do not have enough time, reexamine your thoughts, your beliefs (which are repetitive thoughts), and your inner dialogue as well as your external dialogue. Start retraining your mind to do your bidding and think differently. The habit of thinking negatively is only a habit to change that doesn't require effort, money, or fasting. All you have to do is practice thinking differently, and know that you are the person who controls the thoughts you have; it is something you can do easily.

Chapter Eleven

Parenting

Now let's get a little more practical about time constraints and apply some of these esoteric principles. In child-rearing, we have become a society that has escalated the idea of parenting to a job that is not only impossible but also no fun. Think about what you want your children to experience in life and what skills you want them to have to cope with life. You want them to be successful, which means you want them to experience joy and love to their fullest potential. You also want them to be able to function without you, so they can be independent and share their lives with you—not depend on you for life. The only way that can be done is to show them an example of someone who experiences joy and love to the fullest potential—and someone who is independent of them.

I wonder why we expect our children to follow in our footsteps when we ourselves don't like the footsteps we are making. I wonder why we assume that what we have been taught is correct when we don't see any consistent success with it. I wonder why we waste precious moments with our budding geniuses trying to squash the very genius in them—so they can fit their glorious, multifaceted beings into the square boxes we so graciously provide them.

Show your children someone who has chosen to love them without conditions, and they will grow beyond your wildest expectations. All of the activities you get involved with, the housework you do, and the "quality" time you spend will not do that unless you are a person who can give and live unconditional love. The great majority of children will either become another you or do the opposite. Do you love your life and want your children to be just like you? Do you want them to be exactly opposite? What you really want is for them to become who and what makes them gloriously happy, joyful, and loving, living their unique lives of discovery. If you become who you truly are and love that person, and you do what you truly love, your children will have a much better chance of becoming all they can possibly be.

The practical side of this is to find ways to decrease the time drain that children seem to have become; in other words, stop the insanity. What good is it if you push your child to become a lawyer, and she is not passionate about being a lawyer? You spend the majority of your life at your job; you should be passionate about it. In addition, the most successful people in the world did not get good grades; they simply didn't buy into the judgment of others about their worth. So stop judging your children's success by the grades they get. Let them choose what activities they would like to be in, then discuss how often you would enjoy attending—and be candid about your interests and desires. I don't particularly enjoy spectating, playing video games, and running around outside. I rarely do any of these things, yet my children know I love them intensely.

What are their true needs? I guarantee they don't need you at every function of every activity. Work with other parents to decrease the amount of time you spend running around. Allow your children to do the work, even the work of finding transportation to something they truly want to do—even if they are not completely successful. It is amazing how resourceful they can be when they are motivated by passionate endeavors. Stop worrying about being judged by other parents; the only things you need to provide for your child are food, clothing, shelter, and love—the rest is truly inconsequential. Even children who don't get all of that do well if they want to.

Your children also need downtime, time to be alone and not involved with activities, so they can get in touch with who they are and become creative partners of their own life. Believe that they have a special gift for the world, and they will manifest it. Believe it of yourself, and they will find it easier to manifest. In fact, if you are a huge cheerleader for your children and actually don't believe it with your heart and soul, they will know. It will only serve to make them doubt their worth and depend on external approval instead of having their own magnificent idea of who they are inside themselves. In other words, for praise to work it must be genuine praise; to actually give another true praise, you must be able to praise yourself. True praise and admiration are given from a position of equality, not from a position of diminishing self or others.

Guilt is the surest way for you to be manipulated, and manipulation is a natural survival instinct. Be joyful when your child tries to manipulate you—this means that he or she is a survivor. It will also point you to an area where you have guilt, which you can then get rid of. There is no point to guilt; it always works against you and everyone else. Actually there is one point to guilt—it serves as a guide to go inside and find that ridiculous belief that doesn't serve you in becoming your greatest self.

On the other hand, even as you are joyful that your children are resourceful in the manipulation category, you also want them to become fully actualized. Being fully actualized means being independent of others for their self-worth, energy, motivation, and love. In order to give them that gift, you must first have it yourself. Do not be angry or turned off when a child—or anyone, for that matter—tries to manipulate you. Just don't allow it. This will require you to see, inside yourself, where you need to get rid of your own fears.

A common example is found during divorce. There is so much guilt that children pick up on and use. It is not that they are consciously trying to manipulate. Even so, it is to be seen for the talent it is. Still, the children are sensing something is wrong, and they will try to get their perceived needs met. If a child doesn't pick up any guilt or pity or "this is wrong" vibe, he or she will be quite happy and unaffected. If you look at nature and the history of all civilizations, there is really no wrong way to structure the family—as long as there is love.

This must be clear in your heart, or you will be sending the beacon of guilt out for all who can make use of it: kids, exes, parents, and well-meaning friends. When you see a psychological attack coming your way, realize that you sent the request out, gave the directions, and pulled the trigger. Remove the target from your person, and soon the attacks will stop— and all the people involved will be more at peace and happy. Now, if you are sending out your own attacks, as justified as you may think you are, they will only serve to make things worse for all parties. Even "thoughts" attack—you can act and say the "appropriate" actions and words, yet your thoughts are negative and hostile. In all cases, this will net you negative results. Remember, every negative or judgmental thought toward another will come back to you in short order. It is not about being good; it is about being smart.

Just as an aside about parental involvement: I knew my parents loved me very much, and I did not feel that their love was dependent on whether they came to my activities. In fact, I do not remember them being there most of the time, although my mother would say she was there most of the time. For all I know, they could have been, but I was so busy with my life that I didn't notice. I belonged to a lot of clubs in high school just to get away from home. Though there was love, there were also many conditions, judgments, and drama. I just wanted to be with my peers. I did not care if my parents came to my activities. At that time, they were typically embarrassing to the teenager I was, and that was the simple reality. Just let your children know that you love them in your own way without feeling guilty, and let them grow with that nourishment—children as well as plants can be over-watered but never over-loved. Be genuine about what it is you want, and like, to do with your kids. Don't feel guilt if you are someone who doesn't like to play games or sports like another parent might. This is not necessary; it is not better or worse than another parent's ability—it's just different. If you have a daughter who loves to shop and you don't, don't feel as if you must bond in the shopping mall. You can find other ways to have a relationship. The guidance you need will be how you feel. If it feels like a chore, then something is not right. If it brings you joy and you have a good time, you are going in the right direction.

Your children should also be encouraged to have the same guidance. I wouldn't force my children to spend time with any relative who doesn't stimulate and captivate them. There are no rules that say that you must be good friends with your family members. There is a bond of love, if you are fortunate, but that doesn't necessarily mean that you are friends or share the same interests. I don't obligate my children to attend family functions, but they truly want to go and be a part of these events most of the time. They are encouraged to do what they love, and any help they give is appreciated, just as if a friend was helping out without obligation. Certainly they are part of the household but through no fault of their own. I have given them the example of manifesting a good lifestyle. I do not make my life good because I work hard but rather because I play well and think well and love well.

Teenagers are a great source of growth. Every time I mention that I have a teenager, I get the same reaction: the look of rolled-up eyes, the weary "I know what you are going through." I just can't relate, though, because I see teenagers as such wonderful examples of intensity. They are only problems when we try to control the stallion that is already out of the gate. If you didn't put the posts in well in the first place, then you will have to watch and pray. It is never too late to help them—and yourself—through any ordeal if there is actually a problem, but not the way most think. Stop trying to control and stop the double standards and the judgment, and you have half the battle won. The other half is to actually listen and put yourself in their shoes, knowing full well you can't really wear them.

If you have a lot of judgments about sex or drugs or work or play, you will not be able to see clearly enough to help your teens through the obstacles they will face. If you still think of the world as a hostile, work-oriented, minimally fun place, you will have nothing to give them. They will turn to other teens for help, and you will be out of the loop. If you tell it to them straight, you will have some leverage. That includes telling them that you are still trying to figure life out as well.

You also have to be self-actualized to not have your self-worth attached to how well or how poorly your child does. The job you do as a parent doesn't really matter in the long run. Now, that is a hard pill to swallow. Each child comes into this world unique, with his or her broader perspective etched in. I find consolation in knowing that, from some perspective, they choose the family and parenting they get into, so being who I am should be the best way for them to be who they are. In addition, since there is no manual of parenting that can be accurate for each individual child, it is always a learning process and therefore "mistakes" are acceptable. Lastly, if you look at how people evolve in their lives, you can see success come from the most horrifying childhoods—and horrifying results from the most normal of circumstances. In other words, lighten up; you are doing your best, regardless of what your best is.

When the issue of drugs come up, I tell my kids what the consequences of using them are from a scientific standpoint. I do not use scare tactics. I tell them what the consequences of getting caught using them will be. I also tell them in what way, realistically, they could endanger another while driving, for example. I tell them that using drugs in an adult's house might get that person charged or arrested for giving minors alcohol or drugs. I also give them my thoughts and experiences with drugs, so they have some resources. I encourage them to research anything before they try it, and I make no judgment about it. I ask them to try to think about the worst-case scenario, and if they can live with those consequences, then they are free to act. I honestly think of them as strong individuals who try always to do their best as they explore the world. Since I did some unorthodox exploring in years gone by, I would never think to judge my children or love them less, no matter what.

The issue of sex is another hot topic in the teenage years. Our society has more than double standards about it. In order to bring us back to the issue of having more time, I will say that I feel, at the teenager level, that you can save a lot of time by not trying to fix what isn't broken. Just be available when you can. I personally found that, for a short time, they only need a chauffeur; thus I interpret my role as chauffeur as the perfect time to connect. In this way, I find joy in shuttling my son to and from activities. In finding joy and purpose in that ten or fifteen minutes with my son, it seems like an eternity of meaningful teaching and imparting wisdom. To my son, it just seems like an eternity. All kidding aside though, we get into many interactions and discussions while on those short drives, and I am amazed at what gets accomplished. Whenever you relax into some task and find it joyful and meaningful, it seems to lend life, time, and energy to your life. Life lived with focus on the now, and with your priorities in order, expands your time. Since I am not anxious about getting somewhere or doing something, I am having high-quality time with my child. In fifteen minutes, I can accomplish what may take others weeks or a lifetime of nagging to do.

I don't have an agenda with my children, I just connect to my inner guide. I let the spirit move me. Some may call it riding by the seat of your pants, but it is a good way to ride. All my life, I chastised myself for going with the flow and not being prepared or not planning enough. Who would have thought that it is a good way, just letting the universe do its magic. I do what I can, go where I am most attracted, and get myself out of the way—and magic happens . . . especially now that I don't have guilt about it. It is a funny and ironic principle that when you don't have guilt, there are no negative consequences to an action.

Getting your priorities right is another way to increase time in your life. If you were to lose your child tomorrow, would his dirty room be an issue? How do you want your last moments with your child to be? Does he know you love him beyond words or description? This is my choice, and I am not saying it is right or wrong, but I choose to spend the time with my children with joy and love in my words and heart. Who cares if their shoes are in the middle of the room or if they left the lights on? Close the door of your children's rooms so you don't have to see the mess. No one gets any points that are worth anything for a clean house. I happen to like a clean house and feel better when there is no clutter, but it is not a higher priority than maximizing the smiles and laughter of being with my family.

I don't like actually doing the job of cleaning or organizing, but I like the results if someone else does the work. It is amazing how clutter goes away when you throw things in the trash regularly. Guard your space and time as if your life and the lives of your children depend on it. Allow your children to know that you are human and have likes and dislikes. Allow them to see you have the power to change your life, and they will inherit the same power. Talk to your family about your desires and concerns; you may be surprised to find that they have some ideas that are helpful.

You can apply these ideas to many areas of your life where people you care about are involved. They are sometimes your greatest teachers, showing you where you have work within. They help you find your hot buttons, and as you eliminate the old beliefs, insecurities, and judgments, life starts to flow and time opens up. The time you have is spent doing what you love with people that you love. And yes, you find you have all the time you want for all of it.

Chapter Twelve

Work Smart

I find it amusing when I listen to people complain about others who get preferential treatment at a job or in school. It doesn't matter what those special people do; they get this special consideration, no matter what. These types of complaints support the truth that you create your own reality. The people who believe that they should get special treatment will get it. There is no consideration for worth or whether they deserve it. Instead of complaining about it, learn from it. Instead of complaining to all who will listen that it is not fair, notice that it is consistent with how the universe works. Begin to imagine your requests being handled in the same way. If you think that you have to do twice as much to even consider asking for special consideration, then it will be so. If you still want to hang on to the idea that they are not worthy of the treatment they get, then you will never be worthy of better treatment. Stop comparing, and relax into knowing that you really can't compare accurately anyway. Simply get clear on how you want your life to be, and practice expecting it. Lose the judgment, and get comfortable with the rewards.

I had a friend who was in business for himself. He had a partner who did half the work, took all of her vacation time, and made just as much money. This made him crazy, but she obviously thought she was worth it. She therefore manifested what she wanted. He, on the other hand, worked harder and had less free time. He felt very self-righteous and found many who would agree that he was a much harder worker. Who would you want to be? Do you want to be the one working harder with less free time or the one working less with more free time? Right about now, you are so caught up with judging what is right or wrong, fair or unfair that you couldn't possibly manifest what you want. If you are dependent on the judgment of others, you will be working harder with less free time. If you find yourself bristling with negative emotion because you do not want to be this "slacker," yet you want to have more money and more free time, then listen. Who is the judge that dictates how much work yields how much money? You can always find someone who works harder and makes less money than you. If that is the case, then you are the slacker, aren't you? If, however, you can release your need to judge and compare, you will find yourself working smarter and ending up with more free time. You will have to see it to believe it, but open your mind to the possibility and be prepared for the magic.

If you find that you can never get the work done, always feel pressured to do more, and the more you do, the more you have to do, your time problem is attached to an internal belief. You may even find that you get home late often or have to take work home with you. It may even be that you never feel satisfied with your day and mull over it throughout the evening. It could be that someone else in your work environment is not satisfied with you, and that causes you concern. The internal belief is that you are not good enough, and you are attached to external approval. Instead of putting energy into the nitty-gritty details of it all, put energy into uncovering the false beliefs about life and yourself that hold you in this prison. If you lose the false belief, your external world will reshape itself to accommodate your new beliefs about ease and joy and abundance. You can't have that and still be complaining about slackers and bad management from others.

If you seek external approval, you are seeking your self-worth from a source that will never satisfy you, no matter how hard you work. Even if you are rewarded, you will find a way to make the reward not worth the effort, or you will find that you are constantly running on the treadmill of life. You will not even believe a compliment or encouraging remark. If you do, you may feel as if you must live up to whatever monumental effort you made to gain that moment of approval. You will also live in fear of losing this approval. This is counterproductive if you are trying to expand and free up time to live your life the way you want.

Realize that there is nothing you can do or accomplish that will make you any better than anyone else, and there is nothing you can do or accomplish that will make you any less than anyone else. Start approving of yourself, respecting yourself, allowing yourself to have the life you want. That approval should only hinge on the fact that you exist—and no other criteria. Stop comparing yourself to other people, whether they seem in your opinion to be more or less than you. Keep in the forefront of your thoughts that if you are balanced, relaxed, and happy you will get any job done more efficiently, with higher quality and more rewards for you and the company you work for or for your business. Realize also that how you are treated is a reflection of how you expect to be treated as well as a reflection of what you believe of people and yourself.

Change your beliefs and expectations, and the world around you will change. It is absolutely certain and without exception that this will occur.

In my own life, I had the same problem with the never-ending treadmill. I could never do enough; I never had enough time for everything, and no matter what I did to correct the situation, it always ended up the same. I opened my mind to the possibility that it was my belief that created my problem with time—my belief that I must be extremely busy in order to feel good about myself, to justify the money that I made, and to give myself an excuse to not be perfect. I had to work extremely hard and complain often. I decided to change that belief and make my life easier, because I was tired of the treadmill and could not imagine living the rest of my life that way.

I didn't start out changing my beliefs to change the world around me; I simply wanted to change the way I felt about it. I didn't know that the world around me would change as I changed the beliefs within me. This change in the way I thought and felt caused the world to respond by creating what I wanted to have. I didn't know that this would happen, but it did, much to my surprise. The stronger my beliefs got in my favor, the more my world changed; it was no less than miraculous.

You, too, can change your world in ways that do not involve situations that seem unfairly tilted to your advantage. You see, you create the reality, and you may elevate everyone around you, if they are willing. In other words, if you are afraid that someone will have to work harder to support your "slacking" off, have no fear; it will not happen. In my own experience, no one worked harder because I was working less. I continued to produce as much or more with no struggle because I let go of my need to justify my position with the badge of honor they call "working hard."

Again, there is nothing inherently wrong with hard work, just as there is nothing inherently wrong with having things handed to you on a silver platter. You just have to choose which you want. Once I released my judgments about all of that, I was very sure about how I wanted to live. Having things come easily allows me to joyfully look like I am working really hard while I play at life with lots of time for my family, my passions, and myself.

Chapter Thirteen

People Are a Gift

Becoming aware of how you think and why you act, or for the most part *react*, has a time-saving benefit: you become aware that you are so busy reacting to life that you really are not interested in other people around you. You may put on a good act, even fooling yourself, but if you really think honestly, you are so in need that you can't get past yourself to truly notice others. When you realize this and start filling your own needs, you start becoming aware and genuinely interested in those around you. In that way, you actually network with the human race, which has a ripple effect. People start showing up in your life who can make it easier in a very symbiotic way. Puzzle pieces begin fitting together perfectly.

The truth is, these people were always showing up, but you were missing them, or you were so full of strange and counterproductive beliefs that you couldn't make use of these people—nor could they make use of you. I found a woman right under my nose who took over my household activities and, in addition, loved my children as her own, allowing me to do my calling in a way that was so balanced and comfortable that I am astounded every day still. Up until then, even finding a reliable babysitter had been very difficult. In addition, her attitude of complete satisfaction with her life and joy in her work is a daily inspiration to me.

When you think about it, one of your greatest joys is to be able to make someone's day and connect in meaningful ways with people you love. If you weren't caught up in avoiding the fact that you aren't living the life you want, you would do it often. If you didn't have the thought that there isn't enough time for you to accomplish your self-imposed tasks, you would take time to do it without hesitation. When you are able to stop working at your life and start living it, you will find this happening more and more. The ripple effect then becomes even more evident, and every little smile you give, every moment you spend with someone who needs you, and everything you give to another without the thought of what's in it for you returns to you multiplied beyond belief. If that isn't a savings account for extra time, I don't know what is.

Every person you come in contact with in every moment of your day is the reason for your existence. Each one has a piece of your puzzle and a spark of absolute love that can add to your brightness. Even the person who irritates you, like sand in an oyster, can become a beautiful pearl for you. All you have to do is open your eyes with that in mind. Instead of approaching every situation thinking that you have to defend, prove, or protect yourself, start approaching each situation as the spiritual being you truly are: perfect, magnificent, and unlimited.

Imagine feeling genuine love for all people you come in contact with. What a great way to live! I know it can be done. That feeling you reserve for just a few lucky family members and close friends feels so good. When you can see and feel that for everyone, every aspect and situation in your life takes on new meaning. When you are in love, doesn't time stand still? The same effect happens when you can bring genuine love into every interaction. When you can feel it, not just intellectually say it to yourself, that is when the magic happens. This is what Christ was talking about when he said to love others as you love yourself. I am not religious, and that is not exclusively a

Christian approach; all the spiritual masters have intimated a similar philosophy. But good advice is good advice. Of course, it is not about being good but about being smart. When you have that consciousness, you will see time miracles happen often. Of course, you have to be in love with yourself to be able to love others to that level. Are you in love with yourself?

Chapter Fourteen

To List or Not to List

Let's get back to some practical stuff. The making of lists is one of those suggestions that you hear time and time again. I am here to tell you that lists can work *for* you or *against* you. I do not recommend for or against them. The things that you really want to do will not need a list, and the more you exercise your mind and get rid of the needless clutter in your life, the more you will realize that a list is secondary. I do make use of lists, but I am not dependent on them. I find that writing things down is helpful, but, for the most part, I don't refer to them often or with any pattern. The main point is that you need to trust your own judgment in everything that you do, including getting organized or managing your time.

Don't get attached to how it is "supposed to be done" or how someone else does it. There is no wrong or right way, but there is a way that works for you. Even if your way is not the most efficient way, according to the so-called experts, if it works for you, then that is the way you do it. If it is not working for you, look for a way that attracts you or make up a way that is fun for you. You may even manifest someone in your life who likes to organize things and who will do it for you. I have great people in my business who do what needs to be done very well. They make lists—so I don't have to. I am a bit challenging to work for, but the process is fun and exciting. They seem to enjoy me, and I certainly appreciate and enjoy them.

Making the process work for you is another key component of making time more available for fun and fun more available in your time. When facing a chore or obligation you can't seem to get out of, try making something fun out of it. When doing your business, find ways to make the process a joy. I used to believe that one had to be completely focused on the bottom line, on getting the work done—and save the fun for later as a treat. I would look down my nose at those people goofing off and feel guilty when it was me. Now I find that the bottom line and the work are improved by including the joy and fun as I go. I am having as much fun at work as I am when I go out. The two are blurred into one glorious and joyful experience.

Finding the gifts that every individual has to offer and seeing through to each person's true beauty, in spite of the defenses that block your view, is not only fun, it adds more insight into yourself as well. This exponentially increases your ability to fall in love with *you* as you learn to identify and release your baggage. When you are happy with yourself and clear that you are worthy, you can spend less time thinking about how people think of you or treat you, and whether life is fair; instead, you can concentrate on appreciating the gifts you are being showered with. You can't see them if your attention is on what you don't have or what someone else is getting. Some of my close friends find it difficult to imagine that I actually enjoy the people who have been labeled annoying or weird. When you stop defending yourself and look at these people, taking full responsibility for your feelings, you find that they lead you to places where you have judgment and insecurities or fears. If you follow that lead within, you find the key that honestly releases you from those feelings. Once you can recognize the inner belief or insecurity that makes you choose the emotion of anger or annoyance, sometimes that is all that is necessary to eliminate that experience. You can then go to work enjoying the people you work with without the anger, hostility, annoyance, etc. Now, if you like having all of that drama, annoyance, and pressure at work, then don't do any of the things I say. If you think about it, you may still want a distraction from the fact that you don't like what you do and don't have the strength yet to change that. In that case you may choose to stay angry and annoyed at the people at work. I don't recommend it, but I make no judgments if that is what you want right now. It will not give you more time, however, and it will not change your circumstance for the better.

A woman I know used to brag about her kids and what they were accomplishing. I found this to be annoying and distanced myself from her. When I took full responsibility for my feeling of annoyance, I found that it was rooted in the false belief that I was not being a good mother. I realized that I chose consciously to be the kind of mother I am and that all I need to do is be loving and supportive. I reaffirmed that I know that I am a good mother, and my children are healthy and happy. I revisited my goal for them, which is that they be happy and joyful and free, not attached to accomplishment for their self-worth and not neurotically compelled to "do it all." When I saw this for what it was, I was no longer annoyed by her bragging; in fact, I enjoyed watching her happiness when she spoke of her children and felt closer to her. Our interactions now are beautiful and fun. I can feel love for her and love coming from her to me. Now, that is how I want to live my life. Remember—all your feelings come from you, from what you believe about yourself and the world.

We were talking about lists, weren't we? In summary, let me remind you to use your own intuition, creativity, and choice in how you practically organize your life. You may find lists fun, but I have seen people get addicted, and the list habit controls them instead of helping. When you get rid of your subconscious baggage relating to living your truth, you will not need any organizational tools because your life will be fluid. The brain, which is more powerful than all the computers in the world put together, will not let you forget what you truly want when you allow it to remember.

Chapter Fifteen

Question Everything

In every moment, you are spending your time on, and I would venture to say that you are involved in, activities that you feel you must do. Question that. You do things for your children, significant other, work, social group or friends, and extended family. You may even do community work. You do it the way it has always been done. Question that. You live blindly by rules that have been in place for years, maybe centuries, and that are kept in place by other people living blindly. This blind following or living without awareness keeps you on the path you are on for now. Question that.

What path do you want to take? Is it the fear of a different path that keeps you on the straight and narrow one you walk? Question that fear. If you find one person who has stepped off and lived to tell about it, then your fear is unwarranted. I know there have been many who have stepped off the path and followed the path of their dreams, and they are the only ones who live their greatest potential. They are no different from you—except that they became aware, questioned the norm, and took a step. They made mistakes or, in other words, had learning experiences—and those experiences helped lead them to their greatest joy, to lives lived fully.

The funny thing about walking the straight and narrow, not questioning all things, is that mistakes happen within that path as well. Are there any perfect systems? I rest my case. This is so because we are all unique; a straight and narrow path will be right for only a few. We have been trained to see the mistakes as acceptable and to believe that there is nothing that can be done about it. They are safe mistakes because everyone is making them. Question that. I laugh when people talk about how it was when we were young. Our parents raised us a certain way and now those "values" are being lost. If those methods were good methods then we would all be perfect and living our dream lives . . . are you seeing "perfect"? Is everyone around you?

Questioning all things will not take any effort or time, and it has the potential to give you unlimited time. When you send out a question, the answers start pouring in, provided that you are not entrenched in fear of change. New, more efficient ways of doing things become available. You find strength to see a way to get rid of time-consuming activities that don't serve you and instead, engage in ones that you want. You find excitement and energy at the end of your day that you didn't have before. You find yourself getting up in the morning with thrilled anticipation.

In each area of your life, ask yourself how you would feel if you knew you only had one month, one week, or one day to live. Would you still do certain activities? What if there were no rewards, money, or approval to be gotten from these activities? Would you still do them? What if your actions made no difference to anyone? What if you had all the money in the world? Would you still do the same activities? What if you were absolutely drop-dead gorgeous? Would you still do them? What are you really getting out of doing them?

If you are a spiritual, eternal, perfect being with no limits on what you can create in your life, does that change your perspective? Look through that filter when you are going through your day. It is very freeing to realize that from that perspective, nothing you do really matters—to you or to anyone else. We are all perfect, eternal, spiritual beings without limit. Ten thousand years from now, you will still be that—you and everyone else. This lifetime will be insignificant in the same way that so many moments of your present life are not a part of your memories or awareness. Do you remember what you had for lunch last Wednesday? How about on January 31 of the year you were twelve? If you think about it, most of your life is reduced to a few memories. I am not saying that nothing matters and everything is insignificant, just that you are the one who gives it meaning. Give it the meaning that gives you the greatest pleasure.

Let's say that you choose to experience physical life for the sheer joy of experiencing and rediscovering your creative ability, reconnecting with what is real and infinite. Try seeing your daily life through that filter. What would you do or not do? Since you cannot change your eternal magnificent perfection, all you can do is eternally evolve the experience of it—what fun! Since it is an eternal thing, you have all the time in the world, you can't get it wrong, and you can change direction at any time. You are the one who gets to choose—unless you have allowed someone else or a society or a group to choose for you. Even then, you will figure it out at some point. Why not now?

Who do you spend time with? Do they stimulate you, inspire you, or give you joy? Do you spend time with people because you feel obligated? Do you go to functions because it is expected? What kind of atom bomb would you set off in your small area of influence if you decided to just do what you felt like doing? It is a funny thing that we try to beat that out of our children—their propensity to do what they want to do. I guess we want them to suffer in "prisons" just like we do. We are so afraid to encourage our children to do and be what they want. Wouldn't it be nice to know that when someone was with you, he or she was there purely by choice? That people spend time with you because they want to? And to know that people are doing what they do because they are inspired to do it? You say that isn't real life, but it is real in my life, and I know it can be real in yours if you aren't afraid of your glorious self.

Chapter Sixteen

Getting Control

It seems that a fair amount of stress is related to our lives not going the way we planned or wanted, to the day not going the way we planned, to people not acting the way we wanted. The irony is that the more control you must have, the less you can control your world. When you have no desire or need to control your world or the world of others, you find that you have almost complete control. Needing to control is born of fear, and anything with its roots in fear is going to bring unhappiness and suffering.

So, every time you find your day or life straying from the plan, and this causes you discomfort, ask yourself what your fear is. It could be a subtle judgment about how people should act if they cared, if they were respectful, if they really loved you, if they were useful. All of that becomes the prison you build around yourself. It is very limiting, even if it gives you the illusion of protection for brief periods of time. Many things can provide the illusion of protection. Even the new age movement has its illusions of protection—if you say the right affirmations, have the right attitude, and eat the proper diet, you will be safe. You will have control of your life and nothing "bad" will happen. But life has a way of breaking down our illusions so we can get back to the truth. The only suffering is when people fail to see the truth when their illusions are breaking down and instead choose to focus on the illusion. They suffer because they think the illusion is real—it is not.

The more we try to control something or someone, the more we are controlled by that something or someone. It takes much time, attention, focus, energy, and dedication to control. All of that could be directed toward creating a beautiful and fulfilling life with all the time in the world. I am not saying that one should not make plans, have goals, or want people to act in a certain way—say, for example, respectful or loving. I am not saying that you shouldn't be intense and enthusiastic about those same things. However, if your love of self, idea of who you are, or love of another depends on these things, you are headed for trouble. In addition, if you find negative events in your life, remember that life is a mirror of the sum of our thoughts; look inside, and change your thoughts and beliefs.

Life has a way of guiding us to fulfill our deepest, most heartfelt desires and dreams. If we are really far off the path or have buried these things too deeply, the universe has to push a little harder to get us going in the direction that we really want. Most of us think that fulfilling our purpose will force us to choose between what we want and what this force called the divine, or God, wants, which might mean sacrifice. That is so very far from the truth. The universe or divine intelligence or God has no need for anything here; it wants to fulfill our dreams, love us, and teach us how to use our creative power.

If you are too invested in trying to control the path and events of your life, you will set yourself up for an incredible push, or, worse than that, you will live out your life without your greatest love. I am not talking about a romantic encounter, I am talking about a state of mind that would make you feel as if you were living heaven on earth.

Controlling people in your relationships, whether they are at home, work, or play, actually means that every interaction is a farce. If you must have things your way and control how everything happens, then there is no intimacy and the interaction is rendered null and void. It doesn't count. If you tell your sweetheart that he must call you, and he does, what good is it? If you imply with your actions that there will be hell to pay if he doesn't call, it is meaningless. On the other hand, a spontaneous gesture from that same sweetheart means so very much. It has depth and meaning and intimacy. If you are so busy making everything safe and controlled in your relationship, there will be no room for the spontaneous gesture. Just in case you were wondering, science is providing evidence that intimacy is necessary for health. So is spontaneity and excitement.

In your work, sometimes what looks like failure is exactly what is necessary for your greatest success. Keeping your reins loose and your mind and eyes open gives you the best chance at achieving your dreams, the real ones, with the least amount of struggle. I mention "the real ones" because so many of us think our dreams are something we intellectually choose from the menu society has so neatly put before us. Some of us even pick our dreams based on someone else's dreams or on someone who appears to have what we want. What will make you happier than you ever dreamed possible cannot be found through your intellect. It must be found or verified with your heart and soul. You will know it is right because you will be in a state of ecstasy. Sometimes it is only necessary to know that living that way is possible. It is possible for everyone, not just the lucky few.

Another ironic thing about control is that, at some level, we are directly creating everything that is happening to us or giving away the power to create it. To the degree that you are willing to accept this responsibility without guilt or judgment, that is the degree of ability you will have to create the life you truly want. When you no longer have judgment or guilt, however, you are at a point in life where you are interested in a larger picture. You have mastered your smaller world and are more interested in what your mission is. Your mission is to love, experience, and expand in your personal unique way. To that end, you reach even higher to trust divine guidance. You are no longer seeking things that will not give you what you want. Obviously, this is a big waste of time.

Letting go of the need to control circumstances doesn't mean you won't have goals and plans. You will still make plans and have goals and want particular behavior surrounding you, but without attachment. Like anything in life, it is not control that is harmful but the need to control. The need to control people and situations will consume much time and energy. That need is based in fear and will consume you. If you are in need of controlling someone or something, you cannot be present for your own life. In essence, you have rendered your life nonexistent. In a way, when you are not in touch with the truth inside, you are not living in the moment. The truth inside is what you really want, not what you say to the judging world. Having more time will only happen when you give yourself permission to live your unique life and give everyone else permission to live theirs.

Chapter Seventeen

Defining and Comparing

When you define yourself, you create limits and box yourself in. When you create limits for yourself, you may find that your limited self will have less time. In addition, this false, limited self will have all kinds of baggage that restricts your natural magnificence from full expression. It will also add many hoops for you to jump through to even get to that expression. Sadly, it will hide things from you; you won't even be able to see all the doors out of your small box, because they will be so well hidden.

"I am a stressful person" is a comment I hear often. Stress is a choice you make; it is not a personality trait. There is no genetic predisposition for it. You can learn stressful ways of reacting from your family, but no one is a stressful person by nature. Similarly, feeling that "I am not the expressive type" doesn't mean you can't express yourself; it means you choose not to. You may not be conscious or aware of it. You may not know how to go about being expressive, but by accepting the label, you eliminate the possibility of becoming expressive.

Some people state that they are organized or not organized—again, these are choices we make. Others consider themselves unintelligent or not talented—further self-imposed limitations. There are at least seven different kinds of intelligences and an infinite number of talents. To say that you do not possess these things is to say you have not looked past your nose and you have failed to see your magnificence. It is to say that the universe or God could create something without worth or merit.

Others say that they are not beautiful, but who exactly is the one who defines what is beautiful? What is beautiful to one may not be to another, so we are all beautiful. We all have beauty to the degree that we see beauty.

Another way we define ourselves that further restricts our expression of self is by taking on roles and identifying with them as inherent parts of ourselves. I am a parent, doctor, wife, husband, lawyer, etc. We subconsciously connect our self-worth to our definitions of what our identity is and how much we live up to the definition. The lucky ones at least make up their own definitions; even so, that is limiting. The unlucky ones abide by society's definitions or by their family's definitions or by whatever microcosm they are dependent on.

Each and every one of us is a unique expression of who we are, and we cannot be defined. Even who we were a second ago is slightly different from who we are now. We are many things and no things. Think about how separating these roles are. As a physician, you may feel it inappropriate to show your vulnerability to patients or to supportive staff. You have thus successfully eliminated any real contact with huge groups of people because you have identified yourself with a role and how you think the role ought to be played. If you are unconsciously identifying yourself with a type of people, sometimes referred to as an archetype, you take on all the rules, regulations, and pitfalls this group has.

Every group has its benefits too, but when you become aware of the connection and remove the limitations, you can connect to only the benefits and avoid that which is undesirable to you. For example, as a mother, when you identify with an archetypal mother, you might receive strengths that allow you to stay up long hours, give extraordinary love without much return, and think you are getting incredible gifts. You get support from other mothers and a sense of belonging. The downside is that, in order to be a part of the group, there is an unwritten rule that you must sacrifice self and put your children first. What putting your children first means, however, has become increasingly distorted and expanded to the point that most mothers never regain themselves after the children no longer need them.

Becoming aware allows you to recognize this distortion. Being comfortable with your own idea of self, you will confidently do "motherhood"—or any other role—your own way and avoid the pitfalls. As your child grows, you will reclaim yourself, knowing that this is also what is best for the child. Confidence in your choices will make you immune from criticism. When you truly don't care about other people's opinions, you rarely experience their opinion unless you are interested and ask. Even then you won't feel diminished in any way by their opinion. Your child will have the benefit of a balanced, happy adult as a model in his or her own life. You will also manifest all the time you need and want in your experience of motherhood.

In comparing yourself or your situation to another person or situation, you might be building up the walls of restriction. If that is your intent, or you feel that it is necessary in order for you to be able to grow, then be aware of this. Just as a young child is protected from harm by restrictions, sometimes restrictions can serve a purpose for adults as well. The problem is that most of us become addicted to our restrictions, afraid to go outside the playpen. A healthy child will try to escape the limitations. If you are reading this, my guess is that you are able. Just think about what that means. Everything you have experienced so far in your life hasn't even touched the surface of your potential. You are still in the playpen, just becoming aware that there is a whole other world out there. Just become aware of the kind of freedom you could experience. Freedom from guilt, fear, worry, hurt, and insult. Freedom to create the life you want, with joy and excitement.

Allowing definitions, comparisons, and boundaries to control you and become part of your recognition of self will lead you down a path that inevitably finds you bored, angry, tired, unsatisfied, and blaming others or the world for your situation. It is much more pleasant to enjoy what you are and know you are the best you that can be. There is only one unique you, and no matter how much you embrace that, you will still be magnificent. Rejoice in that. The only question is how much happiness and success and love you are willing to allow and embrace.

Every relationship is unique; every interaction is different. The same interaction between the same people will be different at various times of the day or week. We continue to try to have our relationships follow certain expectations or rules. If we hear that another married couple is having more or less sex than we are, we are quick to evaluate our relationship in light of this information. If our children do not get good grades, we are quick to push them to do better—as if that will make them smarter or increase their chance for success.

Our children are smart already, yet we depend on one grading system that measures one set of parameters to determine our children's intelligence. We are so busy making comparisons and judgments and being disappointed because so many people fail to measure up that we are missing the fun. How many times have you *not* asked someone to spend time with you simply because you always do the asking? You always have a great time and enjoy yourself, but somewhere along the line you decided that it's not fair if you always do the asking. You stop allowing yourself to enjoy the time with this person because you conjured up some rule about who is to ask and how often. Now when you get together, you focus on this thought and miss the jokes and laughter, the love, and possibly the great energy that comes from this person. Maybe you even stop getting together with this person! Another example might be a husband who is not supportive when you're sick but who is great at many other things. Certainly when you were getting together, you didn't notice that aspect of his personality, but as you start to concentrate on his "faults," you start to find more, completely forgetting his positive attributes. Then someone tells you of her good fortune in finding a mate who brings her chicken soup when she's sick, and soon your mate is losing points again. The funny thing is, you don't like chicken soup and prefer to be alone when you're sick. Or maybe you decide that you are an organized person, and you meet someone who throws you off, puts some spontaneity into your life—and all of a sudden, you can't enjoy being with that person because you are "organized" and he is not. Being organized is something you choose to do; it is not who you are, even if we have fallen into the alarming habit of thinking of it that way. If we simply concentrate on what it is we really want in life instead of looking out at what other people want in life, we would not only find life easier but more wonderful—in fact, spectacular.

Looking within, for some reason, is a scary and ambiguous concept. A lot of people talk about doing it, tell people to do it, and expound on the value and benefit of doing it. But the instructions about the nuts and bolts of doing it are usually complicated, shrouded in ritual and mystery, and clouded in the idea that there is something to learn or accomplish. Au contraire! It is a natural state of being, and there is only one requirement—that you exist. Since most of us have grown up in a society that squashes our individuality, intuition, and creativity while rewarding those same traits most handsomely if you can survive the squashing, it is sometimes difficult to realize your own true nature. If you were kept from walking for twenty years, you might find it difficult to do when someone tells you it is your natural way of moving. Once you realized that this was the truth, though, you would find yourself walking quite naturally, even without instruction. If someone were to come to you while you were rediscovering your natural walking potential and that person placed all kinds of rules and regulations on how, where, and when you should walk, you might find that you would never walk. Looking within is the same way. Just *do* it; it is never far from you.

For some, instruction may be helpful, but sometimes an instructor can limit you—or allow you to limit yourself. My point is this: realize that you are to keep your power and that instruction or guidance is just that—guidance! Looking within, finding out who you are, trusting your intuition or inner guidance, and developing a relationship with the divine are natural and easy things to do. You will know you are on the right path simply because it will feel good and it will be easy.

So much of our anxiety is about how well our relationships match up to our expectations and how we match up to the expectations of others. All of these expectations are based on the past, on other people, or on exaggerated stories, insecurities, and the need to control yourself and others. If you stop having any expectations or judgments of yourself or others, you will no longer be a slave to those anxieties.

Get rid of those expectations. I can tell you that I definitely adore and love my children passionately, but I do not enjoy sitting through boring ceremonies for awards. Is there anyone who does? Why do we do it? "Someone," a mythical person who doesn't exist, has made it mandatory for loving parents to go to these affairs. Here's another example: if it didn't matter whether your grown child called you, you would not be offended or even worried if he or she didn't call. You also would know that when he or she did call, he or she really wanted to talk with you and didn't just call out of obligation. On the other hand, not calling you doesn't mean that he or she doesn't love you. I adore my parents, but I have had times in my life when calling them was low on my priority list; I commend their independent spirit—that they didn't wither up and die because I didn't call.

The double standards of life are fascinating; as I mentioned, we squash our individuality, creativity, and intuition, yet we reward most highly those who are creative, individual, and intuitive. We strive to fit in, yet we look up to those who are trendsetters. We are so very attracted to the fringe people but so

very afraid to go there. Even people who go to the fringe set up
their own little microcosm of rules to define how to fit in there.
We envy those who do what they are passionate about, yet we
think it is wrong for us to follow our own passion. Sometimes we
go so far as to think that someone else's passion should be our
own, and when it doesn't quite measure up to what we saw, we
conclude that following passion is not the right path. It *is* the
right path.

If you spend your time trying to live up to ambiguous,
ever-changing definitions or making sure other people are living
up to them so you can be defined by them, your time will be
spent chasing your tail. If you enjoy this activity, then continue,
but then what?

You are a spectacular and amazing being. You are more
than just the person you think you are, and your limitations are
self-imposed. Your passion and purpose in life are meant to be
easy and fun without struggle and effort. Enjoy the adventure
within your magnificent mind and realize that you really can't
do it wrong. Just follow what feels good, and time will expand to
accommodate your new passionate life.

Chapter Eighteen

Loss and Fear

In dealing with my fears and learning detachment, I experienced a period of rapid learning. I took each fear that I could identify and looked at how my experience of life would be, how it would change, and what I would feel if the fear materialized. I discovered that, through each of these things, at least in the imaginary realm, I could deal with it and rediscover a life still filled with joy and purpose. Look at Christopher Reeve and how he found purpose and joy in his situation. I am not even attached to having a great purpose or moving great numbers of people toward higher consciousness. In my world, even the smallest action is as great as the biggest. I don't even judge someone in an "enlightened" state to be better than someone who is filled with struggle or anger or who still must hurt others to find some purpose or relief from pain. At the end of my list, however, I came to the conclusion that out of all the people I was close to and all my fears, my greatest challenge would be losing my sister. She is my soul mate, my best friend, my confidante, and my support. I talked on the phone with her numerous times a week, we spent time together often, and she was the one I turned to when I needed to talk or be refueled. We planned many things for the future while living a great now. We imagined a spa in Hawaii for retirement, made plans to take the kids to different parts of the world to expose them to other cultures, and we wanted to start vacationing together alone—just the two of us—so that we could conquer the world. Being in her presence was one of my greatest joys, and she was really first in my life. I realized that other friends might come and go, lovers may come and go, and my children would move out and get their own lives, but my sister would always be there to share my life in an extraordinary way. So yes, losing her would be my greatest challenge. I did not fear it, however, as I let go of my fears, and I continue to let go of them as they arise. On September 11, 2001, this challenge became a physical reality. My precious sister was on the 104th floor of the WTC when the tragedy occurred.

I found that dealing with my fears in the imaginary realm actually works. I was able to handle that "loss" without stress, depression, pain, or loss of joy. I know this stuff works. I could handle it this way, with joy for her new state of being, and open my eyes to my new state of being because I was already in a state of fearlessness. In order to be in that state, you have to get clear about what you want and what is important to you. She was important to me, and while she lived on earth, I made sure to take advantage of that gift.

I don't question circumstances, as I know all circumstances are for our greatest good. So I know that having her in a different state of being was for our greatest good. Notice I didn't say "losing her," because I don't see it that way. I don't feel it that way. I know we will be in the same state soon anyway, as life is short compared to our reality, which is eternal. I also know that every person chooses his or her entrance and exit, and I honor others' choices, including hers. Lastly, my life is so full of joyful experiences and people that it is overflowing, no matter what happens. In honor of her and myself and all the others I love, I have not felt a need to stop being joyful.

In looking at what I have gained from this experience, I can say that I have closer relationships with my mother and all my friends. There is a piece of my sister in every one of them. I also have a deeper level of freedom and fearlessness. It proves to me, without a shadow of a doubt, that life can be heaven on earth, no matter what the circumstance, if you choose heaven. It also gives me a more real joy in thinking about my own transition and brings tears to my eyes, even now, when I think about seeing her again. What a great gift to have the experience of love that transcends the physical. I am so very thankful.

When I think of my sister and the tears flow, I am not feeling pain but intense love, and I am grateful whenever the love or inspiration is so intense that I feel tears well up in me. That kind of intensity is what I live for, what we all live for—but most are too fearful to experience it.

What does this have to do with having more time in your life? Almost everything. In order to have all the time in your life that you want, you have to be clear about what is important to you and have no fear. When you live life as if each day may be your last day or the last day of someone you love on this earth, you have incredible moments of intense love, and you don't waste time on the things that don't matter. You don't waste your moments feeling pressured or angry or trying to control others; you just love and appreciate all the miracles and gifts before you.

Try going through a day as if you won't be here tomorrow. Try going through a day as if your loved ones won't be here. See if there are millions of things you would do and feel differently. Don't be fearful about it, but appreciate all the gifts you are now seeing that you were missing before. Appreciation makes time expand. Relaxation makes time expand. Love and peace make time expand.

My love goes out to each and every one of you most magnificent, awesome, unlimited, eternal beings that you are, and connected deeply we all are.

Conclusion

Entertain the possibility that you can make time expand and work for you. Become aware of how you think about time, how you speak about time, how you use your time, and what is motivating you. Imagine how you want it to be, and keep developing your amazing imagination.

Get comfortable with doing what you love and making yourself a priority. You may have to change some of your beliefs to get there, and that is possible with a little attention to your motivation.

Don't buy into the illusion of "busy," and breathe. Develop the habit of thinking well of yourself and others. You are a gift to the world and so are they. Remember that the world will reflect what you believe to be true of it, of others, and of yourself.

Enjoy every magnificent moment of your spectacular life as much as possible, and soon your moments will multiply. There is no point to having more uncomfortable time in your life. Until you make your moments fun, joyful, exciting, or relaxing, the universe has no reason to give you more.

Suggested Reading

Books

Thea Alexander	*2150 AD*
Rosemary Altea	*The Eagle and the Rose*
	You Own the Power
Sarah Ban Breathnach	*Something More: Excavating Your Authentic Self*
Joan Borysenko	*The Power of the Mind to Heal*
Deepak Chopra	*Ageless Body, Timeless Mind*
	Path to Love
	Seven Spiritual Laws of Success
	Seven Spiritual Laws of Parenting
	Creative Health
Dalai Lama	*Imagine All the People*
Larry Dossey	*Healing Words: The Power of Prayer and the Practice of Medicine*
Wayne Dyer	*Your Erroneous Zones*
	Pulling Your Own Strings
	The Sky's the Limit
	Real Magic
	You'll See It When You Believe It
	Wisdom of the Ages
Nancy Eos, MD	*Reiki and Medicine*
Clarissa Pinkola Estes	*Women Who Run with Wolves*
Debbie Ford	*The Dark Side of the Light Chasers*
Shakti Gawain	*Living in the Light*

	Creative Visualization
	Return to the Garden
Richard Gerber	*Vibrational Medicine for the 21ˢᵗ Century*
Khalil Gibran	*The Prophet*
Joseph F. Girsone	*Joshua: A Parable for Today*
	Kara: The Lonely Falcon
Neville Goddard	*The Power of Awareness*
	Awakened Imagination
	The Law and the Promise
	At Your Command
Lynn Grasberg	*Bounce Back: The New Play Ethic at Work*
Chris Griscom	*Time Is an Illusion*
Louise Hay	*You Can Heal Your Life*
Ernest Holmes	*Science of Mind*
Peggy Huddleston	*Prepare for Surgery: Faster Healing*
Jon Kabat-Zinn	*Wherever You Go, There You Are*
	Full Catastrophe Living
Byron Katie	*Loving What Is*
Ken Keyes Jr.	*Handbook to Higher Consciousness*
Vasant Lad	*Ayurveda: Science of Self-Healing*
Steven Lewis	*Sanctuary*
Leni Matlin	*Ripples in a Pond*
Robert S. Mendelsohn, MD	*Confessions of a Medical Heretic*
Anita Moorjani	*Dying to Be Me*
Carolyn Myss	*Anatomy of the Spirit: The Seven Stages of Power and Healing*
Mehmet Oz, MD	*Healing from the Heart*
Mary Piper, PhD	*Reviving Ophelia*
James Redfield	*Celestine Prophecy*
	Tenth Insight
Salle Merrill Redfield	*Joy of Meditating*
Jane Roberts	*The Nature of Personal Reality*
	The Unknown Reality
Peter Rosen	*Luminous Life*
Barbara Sher	*I Could Do Anything If I Only Knew What It Was*

Yefim Shubentsov — *Cure Your Cravings*
C. Alexander Simpkins, PhD — *Principles of Meditation*
Robert E. Svoboda — *Hidden Secret of Ayurveda*
Twenty Twenty — *Neville Goddard Simplified*
Joe Vitale — *The AttractorFactor*
Zero Limits
The Awakening Course
Neale Donald Walsh — *Conversations with God I, II, III*
Friendship with God
Carlos Warter — *Recovery of the Sacred*
Andrew Weil — *Eight Weeks to Optimal Health*
Spontaneous Healing
Stuart Wilde — *Silent Power*
Infinite Self
Fred Alan Wolf — *Taking the Quantum Leap*
Gary Zukav — *Dancing Wu Li Masters*
Author Unknown — *Creating Miracles*
A Course in Miracles

Audio Programs

Jay Abraham — *Your Secret Wealth*
Rosemary Altea — *Give the Gift of Healing*
Joan Borysenko, PhD — *Meditation for Self-Healing and Inner Power*
Deepak Chopra — *Magical Mind, Magical Body*
Synchro Destiny
Ageless Body, Timeless Mind
Wayne Dyer — *101 Ways to Transform Your Life*
Through the Wisdom of the Ages
Creating Your World the Way You Really Want It to Be
Carolyn Myss — *Why People Don't Heal and How They Can*
Spiritual Madness

Bernie Seigel — *Healing from the Inside Out*

	Humor and Healing
Dick Sutphen	*Mind Travel*
Stuart Wilde	*Infinite Self*
Marianne Williamson	*Healing*

About the Author

Dr. Edith Behr is a surgeon with a special interest in alternative medicine, especially stress-reduction techniques, which she has incorporated into her practice of medicine for many years.

In addition to her training as a physician and her experience treating patients holistically, she has undertaken a comprehensive study of stress-reduction and life-enhancement methods, techniques, and lifestyles. Dr. Behr has recorded meditation and visualization tapes and has published many articles dealing with stress issues.

Dr. Behr gives seminars and clinics and is available for private sessions. She teaches practical methods of stress reduction to a broad range of personalities. She incorporates a number of methods that are simple to apply, making it possible for anyone, regardless of personal interest or religious or cultural affiliation, to benefit.

Dr. Behr lives and practices medicine in Pottstown, Pennsylvania. She has two sons, Max and Hunter, and five stepchildren, Lindsay, Michael, Jessica, Joseph, and Autumn.

On August 15, 1996, Dr. Behr declared her independence to the universe: "There has to be another way to live! Even though I don't know how to do it yet, I choose to live in joy."

The universe—God, spirit, divine intelligence—stepped into the opening she created with those words, and she began her quest for information. She read many books and listened to many tapes that were recommended to her. And she learned four major concepts that would help her turn her life around.

- All that happens is exactly as it should be. There are no mistakes.
- All personal interactions are exchanges of energy— either giving it or trying to get it.
- There is an infinite source of energy called love. This love is available directly from the source, and it is not necessary to take it from other people.
- We are one with all that is, and the world in which we live is a direct reflection of what is inside us.

Join Dr. Behr as she shares her insights and experiences she's gained since she began this joyful journey in 1996.